RESURRECTING EXCELLENCE

PULPIT & PEW

Jackson W. Carroll, series editor

Pulpit & Pew is a major research project whose purpose is to describe as comprehensively as possible the state of Protestant and Catholic pastoral leadership in the U.S. What are the trends, and what issues do clergy face? The project also aims to contribute to an understanding of excellent pastoral leadership and how it can be called forth and supported. Undertaken by Duke University Divinity School, the project is supported by a grant from Lilly Endowment, Inc. For further information, see *www.pulpitandpew.duke.edu.*

Titles Published

Pastors in Transition: Why Clergy Leave Local Church Ministry
Dean R. Hoge & Jacqueline E. Wenger (2005)

Travelers on the Journey: Pastors Talk About Their Lives and Commitments
Mark D. Constantine (2005)

God's Potters: Pastoral Leadership and the Shaping of Congregations
Jackson W. Carroll (2006)

Resurrecting Excellence: Shaping Faithful Christian Ministry
L. Gregory Jones & Kevin R. Armstrong (2006)

Resurrecting Excellence

Shaping Faithful Christian Ministry

L. Gregory Jones & Kevin R. Armstrong

WILLIAM B. EERDMANS PUBLISHING COMPANY
GRAND RAPIDS, MICHIGAN / CAMBRIDGE, U.K.

Wm. B. Eerdmans Publishing Co.
255 Jefferson Ave. S.E., Grand Rapids, Michigan 49503 /
P.O. Box 163, Cambridge CB3 9PU U.K.

Printed in the United States of America

11 10 09 08 07 06   7 6 5 4 3 2 1

Library of Congress Cataloging-in-Publication Data

Jones, L. Gregory.
   Resurrecting excellence: shaping faithful Christian ministry /
   L. Gregory Jones & Kevin R. Armstrong.
     p.   cm.
   ISBN-10: 0-8028-3234-2 / ISBN-13: 978-0-8028-3234-4 (pbk. : alk. paper)
   1. Pastoral theology.   I. Armstrong, Kevin R.   II. Title.

   BV4011.3.J66 2006
   253 — dc22

                                           2005033666

www.eerdmans.com

For Susan, Nancy, Jenna, Nate, Ben, and Sarah

Contents

Acknowledgments

The authors and publisher gratefully acknowledge permission to reprint material from the works cited below in this volume.

"Who Am I?" by Dietrich Bonhoeffer, from *Letters and Papers from Prison: The Enlarged Edition,* reprinted with the permission of Scribner, an imprint of Simon & Schuster Adult Publishing Group, and © SCM Press, 1971, pp. 347-48. Used by permission.

"They Have Threatened Us with Resurrection," by Julia Esquivel, from *Threatened with Resurrection,* copyright 1994 by The Brethren Press. Used by permission of The Brethren Press, Elgin, Illinois.

"Listen Lord — A Prayer," from *God's Trombones* by James Weldon Johnson, copyright 1927 The Viking Press, Inc., renewed © 1955 by Grace Nail Johnson. Used by permission of Viking Penguin, a division of Penguin Group (USA) Inc.

"The Avowal," by Denise Levertov, from *Oblique Prayers,* copyright © 1984 by Denise Levertov. Reprinted by permission of New Directions Publishing Corp. Reproduced by permission of Pollinger Limited and the proprietor.

"Ask Me," by William Stafford, copyright 1977, 1998 by the Estate of William Stafford. Reprinted from *The Way It Is: New & Selected Poems* with the permission of Graywolf Press, Saint Paul, Minnesota.

"Awful Beautiful Life," words and music by Darryl Worley and Harley Allen, © 2004 EMI April Music Inc., Pittsburg Landing Songs, and Coburn Music Inc./Harley Allen Music (BMI). All rights for Pittsburg Landing Songs controlled and administered by EMI April Music Inc. All rights reserved. International copyright secured. Used by permission.

Introduction

In 2001, Duke Divinity School invited a group of pastors, lay leaders, and theological educators to join a Colloquium on Excellence in Ministry as part of Pulpit & Pew, a research project on the lives and work of American Christian pastoral leaders. Most of the projects within Pulpit & Pew were designed to gather information about clergy in America: what they read, how much they are paid, what their communities expect from them, how they understand their vocation. Our work as a colloquium would be somewhat different. We would ponder the sociological data coming out of the many Pulpit & Pew projects, but we would think about it theologically; we would ask not only what the vocation of ordained Christian ministry looks like in America at the beginning of the twenty-first century but also what pastors and churches and religious communities need to make that vocation a life well lived, a life of creativity, intellectual engagement, and imagination, a life that asks the best of us.

We were lay and ordained, African American, Hispanic, and Anglo. We were male and female, serving in churches large and small, urban and rural, liturgically high and low. We were teachers and administrators in free-standing seminaries, university divinity schools, judicatory offices, and church-related colleges; we were editors (well, one of us was an editor) in religious publishing houses. Although we belonged to congregations and denominations that might identify as "liberal" or "conservative," we found that those categories were too slippery to be helpful in trying to describe ourselves to each other. But theologically we were, shall we say, diverse.

In the midst of all the differences that could have divided us, there was something that we shared, each of us, every one: a love of ministry and a desire for it to be lived well. The pastors among us astounded us time and again by the creativity and imagination with which they approached their work. The lay leaders reminded us consistently that ministry — and the intellectual and spiritual life it requires — belongs to the whole people of God, not just to the ordained. The teachers understood the formation of pastoral leaders and the enrichment of communities of faith as their life's work and longed for ways to articulate the pastoral vocation that would attract people of faithfulness, intelligence, imagination, and courage to embrace it. The editor in our group was as committed to the flourishing of ministry as any of us, and he pushed us to say what we meant in language that was fresh and engaging, language grounded in the traditions of Christianity but not reliant on theological formulae no longer widely shared, language that would make room for new voices to enter the conversation.

Our conversations always seemed to circle back around to the problem of how to give an account of the vocation of pastoral ministry rich enough to hold the joy we sensed in each other's ministries, the intellectual excitement the work of pastoral leadership offers, the compassion and intelligence and creativity the work requires. There are many accounts of ministry, many images, many models, but none of them seemed spacious enough to gather up all we wanted to say. Although we took pleasure in the intellectual challenges of ministry, the image of the "learned minister" seemed too gendered, too quaint. Although we knew the importance of self-knowledge in ministry, and perhaps most especially in the healing dimensions of ministry, the image of the "wounded healer" seemed to require more attention to our own pain than to the healing resources Christian ministry genuinely offers. And although we wholly affirmed the need for excellence in ministry, the professionalized image of the minister as CEO seemed inadequate, viewing children of God as consumers and our ministries as commodities to be shaped and sold in exchange for membership growth and congregational cooperation.

In our desire to develop a new way of narrating the vocation of pastoral ministry, we turned to some old resources. The letters to the Ephesians and the Philippians became very important to us, especially after our colleague, Stephen Fowl, led us in a study of Philippians that profoundly illumined our hopes for and questions about ministry in our own day. Gregory the Great's *Pastoral Care* became a key text, one we returned to again and again. Other touchstones for our conversation included Catherine of Siena's *Dialogue,* the pastoral epistles, the writings of Teresa of Ávila and Martin Luther, and the accounts of ex-slaves who were called to ministry in the midst of the juggernaut of American slavery collected in Clifton Johnson's volume *God Struck Me Dead.* We also engaged contemporary writers and movements, exploring directions and innovations we discovered in diverse settings and denominational traditions. We placed our experiences of pastoral ministry (including our colleague Richard Lischer's written account of his first pastorate in rural Illinois, *Open Secrets*) and the data emerging from Pulpit & Pew into conversation with these older, often less familiar but demanding accounts of ministry and found our imaginations engaged.

During our conversations, we struggled with whether "excellence" is the right word to describe what we wanted to commend in Christian ministry. We eventually agreed that it is an important and life-giving notion, so long as the primary referent for excellence is God. We discussed the importance of excellence as it is patterned in the life, death, and resurrection of Jesus Christ. And we focused on "resurrecting excellence" in order to place the primary accent on the hope and new life of Easter. The image also reminds us of the perennial call to discover in God's excellence a vocation for the life-giving character of Christian discipleship and, more particularly, the vocation of pastoral ministry.

In this book, we have offered an account of the Christian life that invites others to extend the conversation about excellence across time and space — persons considering pastoral ministry as a vocation, students preparing for ministry, pastors and laypersons up to their eyeballs in ministry, judicatory leaders, seminary professors, and communities of faith seeking to strengthen their common life. We hope that there is room enough in this account for pastors and communities from many Christian traditions to find assistance for living more fully into a life of ministry that engages body, mind, and spirit; a life well lived, worthy of life's best energies. If you suspect that pastoral ministry is your vocation, your true work, your calling, we hope this book will give you encouragement to enter fully into a process of discernment, to rise to its challenges with joy. If you are already in ministry, we hope that what we have written will offer a vantage point from which to consider all the many tasks that present themselves to you each day. We hope that it will stimulate you to give your own account of the vocation of ministry, its treasures, its practices, the friendships that sustain it. Indeed, we hope you will find yourself befriended here in a way that matters.

We are particularly indebted to two people whose encouragement and good judgment have helped us with the most difficult chores in writing: knowing how to start and when to end. Stephanie Paulsell was alongside us as we began to craft the original shape of the book. Her clear writing and wisdom still glimmer among these pages. Carol Shoun was gracious and indefatigable as she steered us to the finish, making sure that we said what we meant and meant what we said. Her contributions to the book have been extraordinary.

We are grateful beyond words for the friendship of the participants in the Colloquium on Excellence in Ministry: Edwin Aponte, Michael Joseph Brown, Kyle Childress, Rodney Clapp, Lillian Daniel, Stephen Fowl, Richard Lischer, Stephanie Paulsell, Christine Pohl, Nancy Rich, and Joe Small. These colloquium members were also joined along the way by Ken Carder, Susan Pendleton Jones, Roger Owens, Jack Carroll, Janice Virtue, and Becky McMillan, who each offered a pastor's wisdom, a scholar's judgment, and a friend's confidence. In addition, Ken Carder, Susan Pendleton Jones, and Janice Virtue each read a penultimate draft of the book and offered wise counsel. We thank all of the participants in the colloquium for entrusting us with the task of writing this book, and we hope that we have been able, in some measure, to capture their love of ministry, their joy in their work, and the spirited conversation that we shared.

Finally, we want to thank other groups and individuals whose reading of an early manuscript helped shape and strengthen this book: The Pulpit & Pew National Conference, the Lake Fellows of Second Presbyterian Church in Indianapolis, Richard E. Hamilton, Lisa D. Schubert, Robert Cole, and Craig Dykstra. We are also grateful to Jon Pott and the wonderful folks at Eerdmans, including our editor, Andrew Hoogheem, for their careful attention to the publication of the book.

The time and energy it takes to write a book comes as a gift from hospitable colleagues who consent to our absence, forgive our preoccupations, and graciously attend to those who tap their foot outside our door. We are fortunate for the holy friendships we enjoy at Duke Divinity School and North United Methodist Church in Indianapolis, especially for our administrative assistants, Mary Ann Andrus, Carol Rush, and Mary Beth Ingram.

We have dedicated this book to Susan, Nancy, Jenna, Nate, Ben, and Sarah, who bring Christ to us every day with their laughter, challenge, comfort, and love. We thank God for every day of our life together.

1 Ambition for the Gospel:
A Call to Resurrecting Excellence

As human beings, we long for excellence in our lives and in those with whom we interact. We hope to be treated by an exceptional physician. We desire to learn from a master teacher. We relish the opportunity to hear a gifted musician. We also long for what the Apostle Paul calls "a still more excellent way" in our Christian life and witness.

For Paul, this way of excellence is a way of love patterned in Christ. It is an invitation to a journey, to a way of life with God and others shaped by a love that "is patient . . . kind . . . not envious . . . or arrogant"; that "does not insist on its own way." A love that "never ends" (1 Cor. 13).

This way of life is very different from the world's way, in which excellence is gauged by competition and achievement. Excellence for Paul does not focus on what "I" can do over against others, thereby creating "winners" and "losers." Rather, Paul calls us — as he did the Corinthians — to a way of excelling by embodying God's love manifest in Jesus Christ.

Regrettably, we often lose our way by uncritically adopting worldly understandings. Excellence has become the Holy Grail of American culture. It is the aspiration of the athlete, the benchmark of business and industry, the essence of personal coaching. This culturally conceived excellence is strongly oriented toward success, as evidenced by the thriving "successories" industry that celebrates — and markets — its pursuit. Such "excellence" promotes individual effort and puts a premium on exceptional competence and skill.

In a world of make-or-break rankings, mission statements, and business plans, "excellence" is too often interpreted as the capacity to come out ahead, to exercise strength at the expense of weakness — indeed, to leave encumbering weakness behind. Such interpretation has crept into the church without any adaptation or translation into Christian terms, leading even pastors we would characterize as excellent feeling frustrated. Heidi Neumark writes: "It seems that every time I open a church magazine, I am instructed to raise my expectations, higher and higher. But over the years I have lowered my expectations, and it has made me feel freer and happier. I am more accepting of my limitations and more aware of the grace of God working when I cannot."[1]

If excellence in Christian life is only or even primarily about our expectations and our achievements, then we would agree that there is something dangerous and even perverse about commending excellence. But we also do not think that we are called to lower expectations in order to resist cultural standards of excellence. The alternative to uncritical adoption of cultural standards of excellence is not to reject excellence altogether, nor is to settle for "mediocrity masquerading as faithfulness."[2] Rather, it is an appropriately Christian understanding of excellence.

Ironically, business leaders have recently been mining insights that have long been known to Christians but that we have too often allowed to become obscured by the accretions of contemporary culture. So, for example, business leaders are beginning to talk about the importance of "spirit" in leadership and to pay attention to the good of the larger community rather than individual self-interest. One former CEO, pioneering Dollar General leader Cal Turner Jr., noted to a group of church leaders that he longed for the church to reclaim its insights into Christian leadership and standards of excellence rather than always assuming that it has to learn from business.

Indeed, in our culture it is some business leaders who are helping the church reclaim our understanding of and emphasis on excellence. Jim Collins, for example, begins his important and provocative book *Good to Great* by stressing that the only way we will discover and sus-

---

1. Heidi Neumark, *Breathing Space: A Spiritual Journey in the South Bronx* (Boston: Beacon, 2003), p. 234.
2. We are grateful to John Wimmer for this wonderful phrase.

tain excellence is if we continually highlight its significance. "Good is the enemy of great," he writes. "And that is one of the key reasons why we have so little that becomes great." Too often our sights are set too low, in business as well as in the church.

We might think that Collins would recommend a significant dose of external pressure or competition to create high standards of excellence. But that is to miss the point. On the contrary, Collins suggests that the desire for excellence comes from within: "Those who turn good into great are motivated by a deep *creative* urge and an *inner* compulsion for sheer unadulterated excellence *for its own sake.* Those who perpetuate mediocrity, in contrast, are motivated more by the fear of being left behind."[3]

Collins notes that the best leaders are people who combine a personal humility with a passion for the welfare of the larger organization. And it is at this point, perhaps, that Christians begin to recognize the contours of our own forgotten understanding. We are reminded here of Paul's admonition to the Philippians that, in living lives "worthy of the gospel" (Phil. 1:27), they must look not to their own interests but to the interests of others, must have their passion shaped by witnessing to the extraordinary power of God's inbreaking reign. Paul tells the Philippians to renounce "selfish ambition" (2:3) — that is, self-interested ambition that diminishes and destroys life — suggesting that there is a different kind of ambition — a kingdom-shaped ambition — to which Christians should aspire. And indeed, Paul goes on to describe it: we are to aspire to a life shaped by and patterned in the life, death, and resurrection of Jesus Christ (2:5-11). We are to be ambitious for the gospel.

We will return to this passage in a later section to explore in more detail its implications for the life of Christian excellence. For now, however, let us pause to consider its larger claim. The life, death, and resurrection of Jesus are both the basis and the goal of our summons to excellence. We believe that the resurrection rightly focuses our attention on the hope to which we have been called and shapes our sense of excellence in the light of God's glory as revealed in the crucified and risen Christ. The worthiness — the excellence — of our lives is to be patterned in Christ, and specifically the hope and new life we

3. Jim Collins, *Good to Great* (New York: HarperCollins, 2001), pp. 1, 160.

discover in the power of the resurrection. Our ambition for the gospel is a call to the resurrecting excellence of the Triune God.

We use the term *resurrecting excellence* in this way throughout the book. But there is also another sense in which we use it. We believe that in addition to being resurrected by and to the excellence of Christ, we can participate in the work of "resurrecting" excellence in Christian ministry, for the sake of shaping and nurturing life-giving discipleship and bearing witness to the light of Christ in the world. The task of resurrecting excellence in Christian ministry is a daily renewal of our vocation to bear witness to the new life of Easter. It is also a particularly important task in our culture, where a variety of forces has led us too often to lower our sights and to turn away from being ambitious for the gospel. In order to be about the work of resurrecting excellence, we cannot afford to settle for less than the best that God has entrusted to us. If there is any excellence in Christian life and Christian ministry, anything worthy of praise (Phil. 4:8) — as indeed there is — let us think on these things.

How Do We Measure Christian Excellence?

Christine Pohl challenged our theological colloquium to think carefully about what excellence might mean in a Christian context. She challenged the culturally influenced preoccupation too many have with "human effort, achievement, and perfectly crafted outcomes." By contrast, she offered this wise counsel about Christian excellence:

> Within faithful Christian communities . . . understandings of excellence and practices of excellent ministry will often be complex and somewhat ambiguous given at least the following factors. First, at the center of our proclamation and our hope is a crucified Savior. . . . Second, the Kingdom of God privileges "the poor, crippled, lame, and blind," and faithful followers of Christ have a distinctive call to welcome "the least" to our tables and into our congregations. . . . Third, while pursuing holiness (or excellence), Christians recognize the persistent reality of human sinfulness. We all depend on God's forgiveness and healing as our struggles with sin or its consequences are part of daily congregational life. And finally, our

own motives and efforts in ministry are often a strange mixture of sin and grace, skill and frailty.[4]

Pohl suggests that a Christian understanding of excellence will require distinctive judgments and coherent, theologically grounded standards of evaluation if we are to measure Christian ministry faithfully and well.

Excellence in Christian ministry is perceptible and palpable. Yet it requires a capacity for measuring life by the complexity of judgment and grace as well as the more standard measures of "bodies, budgets, and buildings." The number of people reached in evangelistic efforts and average attendance in worship are certainly important measures of vitality, and so also is the community's rich life in Christ. Excellent ministry may be revealed in the number of mission trips and outreach projects and the amount of money spent in ministry efforts, and it is also revealed by the power and presence of God reflected in signs of forgiveness and gestures of reconciliation.

How do we calculate the effect of reconciling forgiveness, the value of deepened prayer life, the impact of passing on faith to a child, the quiet presence of sitting with a dying parishioner or hammering nails to help provide housing for a homeless family? Such activities are crucial to the way of discipleship, yet they often seem less significant when measured against the ways of the world.

In his memoir *Open Secrets*, Richard Lischer offers an eloquent description of resurrecting excellence in ministry. In particular, he points to his own struggles in reconciling his pastoral ministry in a small congregation in southern Illinois, where very little seemed to be happening, with the televised Watergate hearings in the summer of 1974 that had transfixed the American people. John and Mo Dean seemed to represent real significance, real power in comparison with the Lischers' rather ordinary, prosaic life in ministry in rural Illinois. Lischer struggled with John Dean's power because Dean seemed to have achieved cultural status without ever excelling at anything. Even so, Dean's status had fascinated a nation, and it made Lischer wonder about his life as a pastor. Yet, upon reflection, Lischer affirms the quiet, hidden faithfulness of a pastor's calling:

4. Christine Pohl, "Reflections on Excellent Ministry" (Colloquium on Excellence in Ministry, Duke Divinity School, Durham, N.C., September 27-28, 2001), p. 1.

A minister may drive twenty-five miles to a hospital in order to recite a thirty-second prayer and make the sign of the cross over a comatose parishioner. Who sees this act and judges it to be good? The pastor may devote years of conversation and behind-the-scenes maneuvering in order to promote reconciliation among factions in the community. The preacher may invest fifteen hours of biblical research and reflection on a fifteen-minute speech for no other purpose than to make God a little more believable to the congregation.

Place this near-quixotic pursuit of *souls* beside the creamy power of people like John and Mo, and even a saint will doubt his or her vocation. Does the work of ministry really have the significance we attach to it? What is more important, the political power that openly rules the world, or the kingdom of God that secretly consecrates it?[5]

Perhaps if we articulated a more robust understanding of resurrecting excellence, of genuinely faithful living measured by a sense of what constitutes God's excellence, we would be less likely to doubt our own vocations — whether as laypeople or clergy.

To be sure, the criteria by which we ought to measure Christian life will be qualitative as well as quantitative, and thus difficult to summarize. What if excellence were articulated as a response to the question, "Where is the presence and power of God being manifested in this congregation's life, in this person's life, in this person's pastoral leadership?" In some circumstances the response may draw attention to numerical growth, to new programs and outreach, to expanding financial stewardship, to new and renovated buildings. Yet in other circumstances the response may refer to a pastor's hard work of reconciliation among factions in a community, to a congregation's willingness to care for those who are dying, to a community's persistence in resisting injustice and fostering practices of justice and mercy.

Christian excellence is found in diverse settings and circumstances: in settings of significant numerical growth and evangelistic outreach as well as in quieter settings of faithfulness exercised day by day, week by week. It is found among those who display extraordinary gifts and talents as well as among those who cultivate more limited

5. Richard Lischer, *Open Secrets* (New York: Random House, 2001), pp. 211-12.

gifts and talents in the very best ways possible. There is no one standard or criterion for measuring excellence, other than fidelity to the crucified and risen Christ.

We suggest, then, that the focus should be fixed on how congregations and pastors are bearing witness to the presence and power of God. To be sure, even with such a focus on God there will inevitably be debates and disagreements about the best images of excellence, the appropriate criteria for excellence, and whether particular congregations, laypeople, and clergy merit identification as excellent. Yet while such disagreements and debates are to be expected, a focus on resurrecting excellence will enable both the understanding and the practice of Christian life in general, and of pastoral ministry in particular, to grow in grace and purpose and in beauty in relation to God. We would submit that this last attribute — beauty — may offer the richest understanding of the true measure of Christian excellence.

Excellence as Aesthetic

Christian ministry, lived faithfully and well, is beautiful. This is as true for congregations as it is for the pastors who lead them. It is beautiful to experience or observe the joy, grace, love, mercy, justice, and power that shine forth as people praise God in singing, as they offer hospitality and draw into new life those who have been outsiders, as they pray fervently for one another and for the pains of the community as well as the world, as they learn Scripture and Christian doctrine with one another, as they offer and receive forgiveness, as they resist injustice and foster justice, as they bear witness to the abundance of the Triune God in their vocations in the world.

In order to understand and experience such beauty, we need the "eyes to see" and "ears to hear" that Jesus describes to his disciples in Matthew 13 (vv. 10-17). They are eyes and ears that see and hear as the Triune God sees and hears the lives, hearts, and circumstances of this world that God created and loves so much. As the nineteenth-century Jesuit poet Gerard Manley Hopkins wrote, "The world is charged with the grandeur of God."[6]

---

6. Gerard Manley Hopkins, "God's Grandeur," in *Poems* (London: H. Milford, 1918).

The Reverend John Ames, an elderly Congregationalist minister in Marilynne Robinson's Pulitzer Prize–winning novel *Gilead,* believes that God sees us in aesthetic terms and that we can see God in like terms if we cultivate the capacities to do so. Ames, now in his mid-seventies and reflecting on a lifetime of ministry, has come to the conclusion that *beauty* is at the heart of our relationship with God: "Calvin says somewhere that each of us is an actor on a stage and God is the audience. That metaphor has always interested me, because it makes us artists of our behavior, and the reaction of God to us might be thought of as aesthetic rather than morally judgmental in the ordinary sense."[7]

Ames recalls an old Pentecost sermon in which he proclaimed that it seems as though the Lord occasionally "breathes on this poor gray ember of Creation," turning it briefly to radiance before it recedes back into itself. He now observes, "The Lord is more constant and far more extravagant than [that] seems to imply. Wherever you turn your eyes the world can shine like transfiguration. You don't have to bring a thing to it except a little willingness to see. Only, who could have the courage to see it?"[8]

Who could have the courage to see the world charged with the grandeur of God, to see the world shining like transfiguration? It would be people who have cultivated the wisdom and skill to have eyes to see and ears to hear the beauty of God, the beauty of this world, and the beauty of a congregation's life together. Such wisdom and skill are learned and lived in the friendships and practices of Christian life — because the beauty we are called to see and hear is not culturally defined but rather shaped by the Triune God's abundant, gracious, loving engagement with us and the world.

We begin by describing several congregations and clergy who have eyes to see and ears to hear the gospel-shaped beauty of excellent ministry. They are in diverse geographic and demographic settings, of diverse ethnic constituencies, and affiliated with diverse Christian traditions. What they have in common are the ways in which the beauty of God shines forth in and through their particular contexts. Their stories offer living portraits of beautiful ministry that touch our eyes

7. Marilynne Robinson, *Gilead* (New York: Farrar, Straus & Giroux, 2004), p. 124.
8. Robinson, *Gilead,* p. 245.

and ears and draw us toward God and "the life that really is life" (1 Tim. 6:19).

Portraits of Excellence

Heidi Neumark, pastor of Transfiguration Lutheran Church in the South Bronx for almost two decades, has discovered that a congregation can "shine like transfiguration" even against horrible odds. Transfiguration Lutheran is a Hispanic and African American congregation located in a desperately poor neighborhood in the area where New York City dumps its trash. If Marilynne Robinson's elegant prose and poignant description of John Ames's ministry runs the risk of being dismissed as idealized beauty imagined by a great storyteller, Neumark's memoir, *Breathing Space*, displays the all-too-realistic beauty of ministry cultivated against great odds and in the midst of tremendous suffering.

When Neumark arrives at Transfiguration, the church is on the verge of closing. But Neumark, whose ministry is shaped by the conviction that "love transfigures perception," sees possibility rather than despair — even though despair is far easier to see, to hear, to experience. Neumark insightfully weaves her reflections with diverse threads of learning, from Scripture, St. Augustine, and St. Teresa of Ávila, through sociological, political, and cultural analyses, to writers such as Zora Neale Hurston and Toni Morrison. She also attends to the complex realities and relationships among the people with whom she is in ministry, and in their life together she discovers extraordinary beauty.

One parishioner, Ben, had worked at a florist's on Valentine's Day and the day after to help handle the rush. He was not needed beyond that time, but he had pleaded to work one extra day, a Friday, and be paid only in flowers. He wanted to give the flowers to the church for the worship that Sunday, Transfiguration Sunday. The following week, the church's annual meeting — a time of dealing with "the nitty-gritty of our budget, council elections, deficits, and demons that still drive suffering children into danger, while the disciples stand around worrying how to pay the bills and who is the greatest" — brought the congregation back "down from the mountain."

Yet Neumark's reflection on these two seemingly disparate events illumines the power of having eyes to see and ears to hear. She writes: "We closed our meeting with the Transfiguration prayer, 'Give us the vision to see beyond the turmoil of our world and to behold Jesus in all his glory.' I want to capture every show of glory so that long after the pale yellow orchids of Transfiguration Sunday have faded and disappeared, these words will flower in testimony to Ben's humble goodness and God's mercy. Will a few flowers change the face of the South Bronx? The obvious answer is no. The true answer is yes. It depends on the nature of the flowers."[9]

Neumark not only allows love for her members to transfigure her perception of the church and the community; she reaches out to draw others in. She tells the story of a little boy named Nelson and his siblings and their introduction to Transfiguration.[10] "During one of our Lenten healing services, a little boy named Nelson asked how Jesus knew he was God and how Jesus could be God. Our intern Anita asked him if he was a child of God, and immediately, without missing a beat, Nelson replied, 'Of course I'm a child of God!' But in truth, there was no 'of course' about it."

Nelson had first arrived at the church when he was two, along with twenty other siblings and cousins, all born to either his mother or his aunt. Nelson's mother, who was addicted to drugs but "supposedly managing better than her sister," was caring for her own twelve and some of the cousins, and his grandmother was caring for the rest. They all lived in neighborhood shelters. Neumark notes that as far as she could see, "there was little managing of anything. The children lived in chaos."

> Then all twenty-one began coming to church. . . . They came in and ran wild. They had never been to church before and had no reference points for any expected behavior. Teaching them was fun — but difficult. There were a number of Sundays when I, who happen to have a high tolerance for disorder . . . , guiltily wished they would

9. Neumark, *Breathing Space*, p. 72.

10. We are indebted to Craig Dykstra's commencement address, "Eyes to See, Ears to Hear," delivered at Louisville Presbyterian Theological Seminary, May 22, 2005, for seeing the significance of this story as well as for the broader image of having "eyes to see" and "ears to hear" in relation to Christian ministry.

not come in so I could have some respite from the disruption they created. Some members had that sentiment more frequently. . . . Nevertheless, I was really happy to see the children learning stories about Jesus and singing the songs. We made prayer books together. They did everything with gusto — whether singing God's praises or misbehaving.

After about six months, they were baptized. The waters broke and old Sarah gave birth to all twenty-one. *For the creation waits with eager longing for the revealing of the children of God.* I like the J. B. Phillips translation: *The whole creation is on tiptoe to see the wonderful sight of the children of God coming into their own.* The church was on tiptoe to see this prodigious birth drama, as each fine child left the womb of the font dripping wet, foreheads brightly anointed with the seal of their glorious inheritance. "Of course, I'm a child of God!" said Nelson, and St. Paul adds . . . *if children, then heirs, heirs of God and co-heirs with Christ.* (Romans 8:17)[11]

It was only because Neumark and her congregation had eyes to see and ears to hear that a dysfunctional family of kids could discover that they were "of course" children and thus heirs of God. Neumark notes that "many would consider Nelson and his siblings only as heirs of a family system fraught with abuse and pain, heirs of a cycle that breeds poverty and crime, a future of dry bones."[12] Yet Neumark sees them as children of great promise, dripping wet from the waters of baptism.

In a very different setting, in mostly rural eastern North Carolina, a Roman Catholic priest nicknamed "Padre Pablo" is called to serve the region's growing population of Latino immigrants. Knowing that poor and perhaps illegal immigrants are unlikely to be drawn to a traditional model of church, he goes out to them, meeting them where they are.

One Sunday afternoon he went to a laundromat frequented by Mexican workers and set up a small table. On the table he placed a hand-woven blanket and some bread and wine. That afternoon he

---

11. Neumark, *Breathing Space*, pp. 108-9.
12. Neumark, *Breathing Space*, p. 111.

said mass for five or six people. The numbers grew modestly until soon many were gathering there from various parts of the county. "On some Sundays, the congregants take advantage of a short break in the mass to transfer their clothes from the washers to the dryers. But lately, many of the regulars arrive without their laundry bags. They've come to worship."[13]

Richard Lischer offers this commentary on the story: "The priest is practicing the ministry of reconciliation at its most profound level. For as a servant of the word he is effecting a meeting between the gospel of Jesus Christ and the realities of human existence. In this ministry all the calls converge: the cries of the people, the murmur of his own life, the voice of the church, and the call of God. That it happens quietly among poor people and in an ordinary place is not incidental to the story, but typical of God's grace and the Lord's own freedom for ministry in the world."[14]

Heidi Neumark's and Padre Pablo's ministries are both marked by the act of welcoming strangers, initiating them into the Christian faith, and struggling — often against almost insurmountable odds — to nurture those strangers both in their faith and in their daily lives. Neumark's description of Transfiguration Lutheran Church, like the story of Padre Pablo, brims with theological insight and wisdom. Both pastors pay attention to a world charged with God's grandeur, even in the midst of profound poverty or disadvantage. Both settings reveal lives that are marked by the wounds of suffering. Neumark sees that in the light of Christ's dying and rising, there is beauty in ministry and the congregational life of the body of Christ. It is a dying and rising that shapes a baptismal life. Near the end of her memoir, in a section entitled "And Still We Rise," Neumark reflects on Jesus' wounded body and on the power of his resurrection.

In her concluding section, Neumark describes how the congregation has arisen out of the wounds of suffering, now understood as located in the wounds of Christ. The congregation's life has been trans-

13. We are indebted to Richard Lischer for this story, which he retells in his essay "The Called Life: An Essay on the Pastoral Vocation," *Interpretation* 59 (2005): 175. Lischer's account draws on Yonat Shimron, "Padre Pablo and the Washerette Mass," *Raleigh News and Observer*, September 5, 1997, section E.

14. Lischer, "The Called Life," p. 175.

figured by love, shaping the ways in which Neumark sees her own life as well as those to whom she is deeply connected: "I think the most powerful thing that has happened to me here is that as Transfiguration has seared my soul, I have been irrevocably 'threatened by resurrection.'" The phrase comes from the Guatemalan poet Julia Esquivel, writing beautifully out of her own people's struggles. Neumark closes her account with Esquivel's invitation:

> Join us in this vigil
> and you will know what it is to dream!
> Then you will know how marvelous it is
> to live threatened with Resurrection![15]

These are powerful words that bear witness to ministry that, in the midst of great suffering and woundedness, nonetheless shines forth with the beauty of God's grace seen in the life, death, and resurrection of Christ.

Living threatened with resurrection — it happens in blighted urban areas as well as flourishing suburban communities. The meaning and significance of the resurrection is learned in the beauty of faithful congregational life as well as the beauty and power of doctrine. Faithful preaching can touch the painful wounds of parishioners' encounters with life's living and dying — and bear witness to the hope of living again.

Such was the experience of a large suburban congregation in Indianapolis. Second Presbyterian Church is a growing congregation that for many years was blessed by the leadership of a gifted and learned senior pastor, Dr. William Enright. In a sermon series on the Apostles' Creed, Pastor Enright addressed one clause of the creed each week, focused the congregation's attention on it, and then made vivid for his listeners "the significance and horizons of meaning of each core Christian conviction embedded in the Creed."[16] These convictions

15. Neumark, *Breathing Space*, p. 271. Neumark is quoting Julia Esquivel, "They Have Threatened Us With Resurrection," in *Threatened with Resurrection* (Elgin, Ill.: Brethren, 1994), p. 63.

16. Craig Dykstra first shared this story with the Pulpit & Pew Core Seminar in 2001. We are grateful to him for the use of the story and its retelling. The quotations are from his typescript of the story.

were not expressed as otherworldly ideals but were directly connected to the shape of an individual's life as well as the life of the community of faith.

The series continued through fall and winter into Lent, each Sunday the congregation standing to recite the Creed with increasing conviction. "We no longer bent over, mumbling something we didn't understand or really much care about. Instead, week by week, we stood up straighter and stronger until, finally, we almost sang it out together."

The christological clauses were the focus of Advent. The Passion clauses were explored in Easter. For many, the most memorable sermon was the one on "the resurrection of the body and the life everlasting." The pastor crafted a theologically and biblically rich sermon connecting the blessedness of being God's creatures with the Christian hope in the resurrection. The sermon was significant in itself, but the congregation also knew it was grounded in a significant moment of the previous week.

A middle-aged member of Second Presbyterian was living with a debilitating neurological illness that had slowly rendered him virtually immobilized. Communication was possible only with a highly sophisticated electronic device that enabled him to write — one letter at a time — by winking.

The man and his family knew that the end of life would likely come through suffocation as his throat and lungs eventually collapsed. As the inevitable approached, Pastor Enright was asked to help the man and his family make a decision. There were two questions: Is it suicide to remove life support mechanisms? And should this man and his family take such a step?

Pastor Enright clearly stated his position that to turn off the machines would not be suicide. He also said that determining what to do and when to do it was a decision for the man and his family, but he promised that if they decided to remove life support, he would be there at every step along the way. In time, they indeed reached that decision and set a date.

On the Sunday evening before the life support was to be removed, the man was carried on a bed into the sanctuary where he took Communion with the rest of the congregation. On the appointed day later that week, a community of caregivers, family, and friends gathered around him. Pastor Enright led the gathered company in prayer and the singing of hymns. A sedative was given, the machines were turned off, and the man died in the midst of tears and blessing.

The following Sunday, the story of this decision and death was told as part of the sermon on "the resurrection of the body and the life everlasting." The family of the man who died was sitting in the front pew. After the sermon, the family and congregation rose together and with tear-filled eyes recited again the Creed that had come to mean so much more to them: "I believe . . . in the resurrection of the body and the life everlasting." That conviction made it possible to let go of life as their loved one had done, and as they affirmed that they all would one day need to do.

William Enright displays the beauty of ministry as it is lived in and through the challenges of day-to-day life. He is able to draw together a lifetime of study, an appreciation of Scripture and doctrine illumined in preaching, and a compassion that emerges from patterning one's own life in Christ's dying and rising. He understands what it means to practice the beauty of God's grace and love in the company of the whole people of God, directing the diversity of his tasks to building up the body of Christ — and thereby living "threatened with resurrection."

William Enright reminded his congregation, and us, that our strength and the strength of a community are deeply connected. Individually regarded by God, we are still called to be saints and priests together. Crafting that kind of covenant among the people of God is always challenging, and very often costly, but it is also a bold and vibrant witness to the world that "we do not live to ourselves, and we do not die to ourselves. If we live, we live to the Lord, and if we die, we die to the Lord; so then, whether we live or whether we die, we are the Lord's" (Rom. 14:7-8). It is in this supreme act of obedience and self-emptying that we discover the fullness of God's love.

The transformative power of such dying and rising can be seen in the story of a small, stagnant congregation in an area that didn't seem fertile for growth. Antioch Christian Church has been located in a small county-seat town in southern Indiana since 1867. The county's population is growing less than 1 percent each year. About two-thirds of the adult population have a high school diploma; less than 8 percent are college graduates. The poverty level is 14 percent, and less than half the population claims a church home. Not exactly the kind of place where one would expect a church to grow from 100 people to 1,100 in ten years. But that is exactly what happened.[17]

In 1994, about 100 names were on the membership roll at Antioch. The church was in a remote location, and the congregation was persuaded that if they were to witness to the unchurched, they would have to go where they could be seen. Church leaders made the difficult decision to move.

A longtime member of the congregation had been politely asking whether a decision to move might be delayed until her death. When she broached the subject with her son, who happened to be a church elder, he answered, "Mom, if we wait until you die to move, the entire church might be dead." "Well," she said, "then let's go!"

So, in the spring of 1994, Antioch followed that rallying cry in a memorable Easter celebration. Services began in the old building to celebrate and honor the past. Then 65 men, women, and children moved into their future, driving one last time down the dusty, gravel road from their old building to the new facility located near the town, on the highway. "It was all an obvious celebration of Christ's resurrection," wrote Pastor Alan Scott, "and the resurrection of what had once been labeled a dying church."

Members believe that fervent prayer has allowed them to reach their neighbors in the county and the surrounding area. Before each meeting, for example, the elders of the church pray for three-quarters of an hour and study the Bible for an hour and a half. They are the congregation's spiritual leaders, Scott says, and set the example for other members.

Antioch's move was accompanied by a commitment to worship, faithfulness, and spiritual giftedness. Believing that God's Spirit was already poured out on the county's population, for whom they had been praying, Antioch's members reached out to their neighbors and invited them to discover the gifts that God had already given them. "If you would visit Antioch," says the pastor, "you would immediately see many spots of imperfection, but you would also see passionate people who are trying to give God their best because their best is a reflection of an excellent God."

17. We are grateful to Alan Scott for sharing this story with us.

We describe these congregations and pastoral leaders as engaged in beautiful ministry because we see the gospel shine forth in their life and work. They cultivate faithfulness in diverse contexts, with diverse people, in diverse ways, but with a common commitment to "live your life in a manner worthy of the gospel of Christ" (Phil. 1:27). Having glimpsed the glory of God, they seek to reflect that beauty by the power of the Spirit conforming them to Christ. Indeed, Paul's letter to the Philippians provides an instructive lens for understanding the shape of these examples of beautiful ministry, and of the kind of ministry we commend in this book.

Philippians: A Theology of Christian Excellence

Philippians characterizes the significance of ministry shaped by God's abundant grace revealed in the crucified and risen Christ. We are called to develop a common life that strives "side by side with one mind for the faith of the gospel" (Phil. 1:27), in difficult as well as good times, in suffering as well as triumph. We are called to cultivate a common life marked by the "mind of Christ" (see Phil. 2:5). What is that mind? It is the mind of the One

> who, though he was in the form of God,
> > did not regard equality with God
> > as something to be exploited,
> but emptied himself,
> > taking the form of a slave,
> > being born in human likeness.
> And being found in human form,
> > he humbled himself
> > and became obedient to the point of death —
> > even death on a cross.
> Therefore God also highly exalted him
> > and gave him the name
> > that is above every name,
> so that at the name of Jesus

> every knee should bend,
> in heaven and on earth and under the earth,
> and every tongue should confess
> that Jesus Christ is Lord,
> to the glory of God the Father. (Phil. 2:6-11)

This is an extraordinary passage with rich implications for shaping faithful Christian living. Yet some of those implications may not be immediately apparent.

First, it is important to note that seeking insight into Christ's mind is not simply a matter of cognitive reasoning. The Greek word *phronein*, which appears in verse 5 ("let this *mind* be in you"), is better construed as a form of practical reasoning that involves our whole lives: feeling, thinking, and perceiving, as well as acting and living. Stephen Fowl, a member of our theological colloquium who guided our discussion of Philippians, captures the force of this insight in his translation: "Let this be your pattern of thinking, acting, and feeling, which was also displayed in Christ Jesus."[18]

A second implication concerns the intended recipients of Paul's instruction. The Greek for the second person address in the passage, "you" in many translations and "your" in Fowl's, is not singular but plural. Paul is calling the Christians at Philippi to develop this pattern of practical reasoning, this discernment, as a community. We depend on networks of mutuality, of holy friendships, to cultivate wise and faithful habits of feeling, thinking, and acting both for the community and for our own vocational direction.[19]

Third, it is clear, especially from verses 9-11, that we cannot do exactly what Jesus did — nor are we called to do so.[20] Rather, as Fowl's

---

18. Stephen Fowl, *Philippians* (Grand Rapids: Eerdmans, 2006), p. 88.

19. Fowl notes in his commentary, and develops in very suggestive ways, the significance of friendship in Philippians. See especially Part III, "Theological Horizons of Philippians."

20. We also do not want to endorse the ways in which the cross has too often become a symbol for the peculiar kind of masochistic suffering that certain Christians — and particularly the clergy — are sometimes expected to embrace in their vocations. There has too often been a tendency to give the clergy implicit, and sometimes explicit, messages that they are called to suffer and sacrifice in ways not expected of laity. Such expectations of self-sacrifice arise from a distorted and destructive set of understand-

translation of verse 5 illumines, we are to develop patterns of feeling, thinking, and acting that are conformed to the pattern of Christ's dying and rising. In Fowl's words, "the story of Christ in 2:6-11 functions as an exemplar for Christians from which they can draw analogies to their own situations in order to order their common life in a manner worthy of the gospel."[21]

We glimpsed in the stories of the pastors and their congregations the cultivation of such a common life marked by Christ's dying and rising. It involves being called into community through evangelism and faithful discernment, being educated and formed in the gospel through powerful preaching and teaching, and being shaped for faithful Christian witness in the world through holy friendships marked by blessing, accountability, and abundant grace. It involves cultivating eyes to see and ears to hear, by the power of the Spirit, God's work in the world and in people's lives.

Insofar as Christians display in congregational life the pattern of feeling, thinking, and acting that was displayed in Christ Jesus, there will be profound beauty in our life together. For, as Fowl notes, "the claim that Christ was in the 'form' of God [2:6] can be taken as a reference to Christ's sharing in the eternal glory of God and making that glory visible. It may *also* indicate that the best way to think of Christ's manifestation of the glory of God is in terms of Christ's beautiful body, a beauty that is not diminished but enhanced by taking on the 'form' of a slave."[22]

---

ings. These invocations of "self-sacrifice" have also been the subject of criticism of some understandings of the atonement by both feminists and womanists who suggest that oppressed people are often called to further their oppression by taking up crosses and sacrificing themselves. See Joanne Carlson Brown and Rebecca Parker, "For God So Loved the World?" in *Christianity, Patriarchy, and Abuse,* ed. Joanne Carlson Brown and Carole R. Bohn (New York: Pilgrim, 1989); also Delores S. Williams, *Sisters in the Wilderness* (Maryknoll, N.Y.: Orbis, 1993). We understand the perspectives that give rise to this criticism — whether from clergy, women, African Americans, or any other group that is singled out for suffering and oppression. However, our point is that this is a distortion of the richness of cruciform living, and our aim in this book is to help illumine how the cross and cruciform living are inextricably linked to resurrecting excellence. We commend an understanding of the cross that is grounded in the self-emptying, life-giving character of Jesus's life, death, and resurrection.

21. Fowl, *Philippians,* p. 106.
22. Fowl, *Philippians,* p. 94. Fowl connects this interpretation to the following

Two further points are important to note in relation to Philippians. First, our stories are not simply "illustrations" of the conceptual argument of the book. Rather, they are crucial embodiments that help us learn how to draw analogical connections to Christ's dying and rising. Fowl's comment on Philippians 2:19-30 is instructive:

> If we understand saints as those who have masterfully lived in a manner worthy of the gospel of Christ, those who have achieved excellence in the performance of Scripture, then their lives should play an important regulative and disciplining role in our lives. Neither the story of Christ nor Scripture in its fullness are self-interpreting. If Christians are to interpret and embody these texts in the concrete situations in which they find themselves (which is precisely what Paul wants the Philippians to do), then we must attend to those saintly lives around us as well as those saints preceding us who best embody those texts.[23]

We are not suggesting that some extraordinarily high bar must be met in order for stories to play a crucial exemplary role. But we do need examples, both those who have most faithfully lived out Christian ministry, tested over time, as well as those whose contemporary stories illumine particular aspects of our yearning to discover the beauty and power of Christian life.

Second, beautiful ministry both calls forth and demands the very best we can provide; it calls for excellence in all that we are and do. Philippians is marked by both abundant grace and a sense of the stakes involved in faithfully following Christ in the power of the Holy Spirit: the high calling from God to live our lives in a manner worthy of the gospel, the encouragement to be ambitious for the gospel, the injunction to let the pattern of our feeling, thinking, and acting be the

---

comment by Bernard of Clairvaux, from his homilies on the Song of Songs: "How beautiful you appear to the angels, Lord Jesus, in the form of God, eternal, begotten before the daystar amid the splendors of heaven, the radiant light of God's glory and the perfect copy of his nature, the unchanging and untarnished brightness of eternal life! How beautiful you are to me, my Lord, even in the very discarding of your beauty! When you divested yourself of the native radiance of the unfailing light, then your kindness was thrown into relief, your love shone out more brightly . . ." (*On the Song of Songs* 49.5).

23. Fowl, *Philippians*, p. 142.

same as was displayed in Christ Jesus, and the challenge to develop analogical means of patterning our own lives in Christ in the particular situations in which we find ourselves. So, in chapter 4, Paul enjoins the Philippians to focus their attention on "any excellence" and "anything worthy of praise" (4:8).

This suggests that in Philippians, beautiful ministry is inspired by and inspires standards of excellence. Learning to attend to God's beauty and to see and hear through God-inspired eyes and ears calls forth the strongest patterns of feeling, thinking, and acting. But this is an excellence that is not about our efforts or culturally defined expectations. Rather, it is an excellence that is shaped by God's excellence, nurtured by the new life in Christ to which we are all called in the power of the Holy Spirit.

Contemporary Challenges and Opportunities for Christian Ministry

We believe that there is a yearning in people's hearts to develop eyes to see and ears to hear the beauty of God's grace and love in the world as well as in their own lives. We find this yearning for a life well lived among Christians as well as restless seekers. It is a yearning that searches for new life, that longs to experience a sense of flourishing intrinsically linked to excellence. It is a yearning that Paul takes up with the Philippians, and also with us. It is a yearning for beauty and excellence that has the Triune God as its referent, standard, and source.

When people discover and experience the beauty of an excellent Christian congregation, they are drawn to reorder their lives to become part of it. By participating in such a congregation, people begin to learn to cast off sinful habits that have wreaked havoc in their lives and in the world, they cultivate practices and friendships that bear witness to the light of Christ by the power of the Spirit, and they shift their priorities so that this congregation becomes the primary marker by which they order their days.

Such congregations are typically blessed by excellent pastoral leadership. They have leaders who have helped to cultivate the passions and commitments that now animate congregational life. In turn, such congregations appreciate, support, and emphasize the importance of

Christian excellence in pastoral leadership. Over time, profound synergies develop between vital congregations and excellent pastors, creating spirals in which congregations, pastors, and wider communities flourish in beautiful ways. Excellent pastors are gifted at calling laity to vital discipleship and helping them live their vocations faithfully in the world, in educating their congregations through theological leadership in worship and teaching, and in shaping a vision for a way of life that reaches beyond the walls of the church. Strong congregations cultivate a life together that inspires and requires gifted pastoral leadership, taking risks and posing questions that raise the standards for what is possible and needed for the life of the community.

We have ourselves been shaped by this kind of ministry, by the standards of Christian excellence in vital congregations and faithful pastoral leaders. We have dedicated our own lives to this ministry because we have beheld the beauty of the Triune God in and through these communities and their leaders and have discerned a vocation to participate in the high calling of ordained pastoral leadership.

Yet we are also painfully aware that while there are many excellent Christian congregations and pastoral leaders, there are not enough of them. Too many people yearning to experience a life well lived, people who have glimpsed the beauty, truth, and goodness of God, have experienced congregations and pastoral leaders that are marked either by destructiveness and corruption or by mediocrity. These congregations and pastors seem stuck in destructive patterns of fear, hostility, and bitterness or, perhaps because previous dreams have failed, have settled for maintenance of the status quo rather than seeking to bear witness to the Holy Spirit who, in conforming the world to Christ, is "making all things new" (Rev. 21:5).

Just as vital congregations and effective pastors together create synergistic spirals of beauty and vitality and flourishing lives, weak congregations and problematic pastors create degenerative spirals. Some congregations have become pathologically turned in on themselves, intent more on sustaining patterns of brokenness and antagonism that reflect division and discord than on building a common life marked by Christ.[24] And some congregations have become so accom-

---

24. To be sure, there is an enormous issue we do not take up in this context: the scandal of brokenness and disunity in the whole body of Christ, the Church of Jesus

modated to cultural standards that they fail to open themselves up to the power of the Holy Spirit.

Further, there are congregations that are known for destroying the spirit of the pastors who are called to lead them. They do this sometimes through impossible expectations, at other times through passive-aggressive subversions, and often by subtle clues that the pastor had better not try to change anything in the congregation.

Congregations are not the only problem. Destructive leadership or, worse, moral turpitude can cause brokenness and cynicism in congregations — often for years after the event or after the pastoral leader who exhibited these characteristics has departed. Damaged trust can also make it more difficult for persons to believe in God and to hope that the church can make a positive difference in their lives. While all Christians are called to holy living, those entrusted with pastoral leadership have a special obligation to be faithful shepherds of the flock.

The sixth-century pope and theologian Gregory the Great offers a poignant image of the damage that happens from destructive pastoral leadership. He notes that when the pastor "walks through steep places, the flock following him comes to a precipice." He goes on to cite several passages from the Old Testament, noting that "the Lord says by the Prophet concerning the priests: 'They were a stumbling block of iniquity to the house of Israel'" (Ezek. 44:12). Gregory then concludes: "For no one does more harm in the Church than he, who having the title or rank of holiness, acts evilly."[25]

Mediocrity masquerading as faithfulness is equally problematic for both congregations and pastoral leaders. When congregations and their pastoral leaders settle for the conviction that not much should be expected to happen, sights are lowered and expectations are dimin-

---

Christ. This has profound and painful implications for the faithfulness of congregations and pastors, but it is beyond the scope of the present volume. Ephraim Radner has posed a powerful challenge to the churches to address our scandalous divisions in his book *The End of the Church: A Pneumatology of Christian Division in the West* (Grand Rapids: Eerdmans, 1998). Our aim here is more modest: to commend patterns of excellence in ministry that we hope will be generative for a fairly wide ecumenical audience, while nonetheless acknowledging that there are painful differences — even in the conceptions and ordering of ministry — that we do not address.

25. Gregory the Great, *Pastoral Care*, trans. Henry Davis, S.J. (New York: Newman, 1950), 1.2, p. 24.

ished. Rather than the abrupt sinful brokenness found in congregational divisions and destructive leadership, mediocre congregations and pastors betray the gospel by failing to trust in the transformative, life-giving power of the Triune God's abundant grace and love. Mediocrity creates a slower spiral downward than outright corruption, but death and destruction are no less likely to occur. It just takes more time.

Unfortunately, many people in contemporary America are increasingly convinced that Christianity is marked more by destructive congregations and leaders or, at the very least, mediocre congregations and leaders, than by vibrant examples of beautiful and excellent Christian life. Ironically, this growing conviction is emerging at the same time that we are seeing heightened signs of both a yearning for the gospel and a need for its healing and transforming power.

This has become particularly poignant in reflection about the quality of pastoral leadership in the United States, a primary focus of this book. We believe that you cannot adequately address pastoral leadership apart from congregations and their day-to-day lives, hopes and fears, joys and griefs. Yet we believe that there are peculiar challenges and opportunities for pastoral leadership in the high calling of equipping the saints for ministry (see Eph. 4:12), and we are concerned that despite the yearning and the need, the church does not have the quality of pastoral leadership it needs.

We cannot address this concern about quality on simply an individual basis. While it is true that too many individual pastors have betrayed the trust of God and their congregations through inappropriate behavior, there is equally troubling evidence of low morale and burnout among clergy. The latter challenges have less to do with individuals and their calling than with broader structural and systemic conditions of contemporary pastoral leadership across denominations. Important dimensions of these conditions have emerged in research conducted by Duke Divinity School's Pulpit & Pew project, as well as others: an often desperate sense of loneliness, a high dropout rate in the first five years of ministry, personal financial struggles because of the problematic changes in the economics of ministry, splits within congregations as well as denominations, the loss of a sense of purpose that leads to thinking of pastoral ministry as little more than a low-paying job, and a reluctance to encourage others to consider pastoral leadership as a vocation. The quality of those entering the ministry seems to have declined relative to other vocations. Ordained ministry's status as a respected and trustworthy vocation has also declined in the broader culture. We believe that this has less to do with evildoing (problematic though that is) and more to do with mediocrity among both congregations and clergy, and in the processes by which people are identified (or identify themselves) for pastoral leadership.

Further, clergy find themselves distracted by so many different tasks that it is difficult for them to know when they are truly fulfilling their calling. The nineteenth-century novelist George Eliot called this being "dispersed among hindrances." Rodney Clapp described it to our colloquium as feeling not so much "spread thin" as "crushed thin." Richard Lischer calls it being "sliced, diced, and cubed into a thousand contacts and competencies but left without a heart of passion in the word, without a vocation."[26]

These structural and systemic conditions for pastoral leadership have often left clergy confused about their work and disconnected from their vocation. Indeed, in a national clergy survey in 2001 conducted by Pulpit & Pew, over half of the clergy across the denominations reported that among their greatest problems is their "difficulty reaching people with the gospel today." In part, this undoubtedly has to do with impoverished dispositions and habits of feeling, thinking, and acting. In part, we American Christians have not done as good a job in educative formation for all Christians as we should, the kind of formation that would enable people to be nurtured in the gospel in powerful, imaginative ways. But can we expect clergy to be able to fulfill their vocation if they are disconnected from it or have at best a distorted conception of it?

For a variety of reasons, pastoral leadership does not seem to offer the promise of a life well lived. Yet the same clergy in the 2001 survey reported that they see pastoral leadership as a profoundly satisfying vocation. How could this be? Might it be that clergy find pastoral leadership to be satisfying in principle (when ministry is at its best) in

26. George Eliot, *Middlemarch* (1871; Oxford: Oxford University Press, 1997), p. 4; Rodney Clapp, "Providence and the Office of Ministry" (Colloquium on Excellence in Ministry, Duke Divinity School, Durham, N.C., April 25, 2003), p. 2; Richard Lischer, "The Called Life," p. 168.

spite of the enormous challenges and systemic distortions that make it so difficult to experience in daily life? Might we be able to reclaim a sense of Christian ministry at its best — in which congregations and clergy together manifest the abundant, life-giving presence of God in Jesus Christ — if we address the pathologies that make it difficult for people to provide faithful and effective pastoral leadership?

We believe that diverse pathologies afflicting contemporary ministry need to be addressed, and we will be touching on them throughout the book. Even so, we are convinced that underlying the particular pathologies that beset contemporary pastoral leadership is a crisis of confidence that Christian life in general, and pastoral leadership in particular, has a *telos*, a direction and purpose. As a result, pastoral leaders are caught by larger cultural systems, outdated conceptions of maintaining and managing a disappearing religious establishment, or the competing and often incompatible expectations among diverse laypeople, judicatory leaders, peer clergy, and the pastors' own interior sense of what they are called to be doing.

In the marketplace of professions, clergy often feel as if they are amateur, second-rate versions of more distinguished vocations: therapists, but not quite what doctors and nurses are; teachers, but not quite what scholars and professors are; leaders, but not quite what politicians and business executives are; communicators, but not quite what performers and writers are. Unsure of their own vocation, they too often become what Stanley Hauerwas has characterized as "quivering masses of availability." To many distressed and discouraged Christians, laity and clergy alike, the job description for ordained ministry reads like a depressing want ad:

> WANTED: Person to fill position that involves important but undervalued work; exact job description unclear. Long hours; must work weekends and holidays. Low pay. Master's degree required; doctorate preferred. Must be accomplished at multitasking, including running an organization without clear authority to do so. The successful candidate will be skilled as a public speaker, manager, politician, and therapist, and will devote significant time each week to pastoral visits. The position reports to multiple bosses.

Why would anyone want to undertake such work?

From this perspective, we should not be surprised to discover fewer people wanting to enter ordained ministry — it looks to be a recipe for vocational frustration and self-destruction.

What if, by contrast, the description read as follows?

> WANTED: Persons for a vocation that leads God's people in bearing witness to God's new creation revealed in Jesus Christ by the power of the Holy Spirit. Work schedule is shaped by relationships, focusing on what is important in people's lives, and depends on regular rhythms of work, rest, and play. Compensation is shaped by a mutual discernment of what is necessary in order for the persons (and, where appropriate, their families) to have an appropriately well-lived life. The vocation involves cultivating holy dispositions, preaching and teaching, nurturing rigorous study, and shaping practices of faithful living in church and world. Lifelong education and formation is expected in order to enable others also to grow throughout their lives. The successful candidate will collaborate with others toward the same ends. The vocation reports to God.

Such a description sounds like an invitation into an adventuresome, life-giving journey of leadership to which many would be attracted. It is, indeed, a description that has been at the heart of the best understandings of ordained pastoral leadership through the centuries. Pastoral leadership, on this understanding, is both inviting and worthy.

In order to cultivate such an understanding of pastoral leadership, and of Christian life more generally, we need to discover afresh the "still more excellent way" of love that leads us toward the *telos*, the goal, of God's reign in its fullness. The more excellent way is patterned in the crucified and risen Christ. Along this way, we discover intersections that draw together people, practices, and understandings — unlike the way of the world, which tends toward separations and oppositions. Life and love patterned in Christ is, indeed, a still more excellent way.

2 *Inhabiting the Intersections: A Still More Excellent Way*

Since 1920, North United Methodist Church in Indianapolis has been located at one of the most visible and variegated intersections in the city. The state's governor lives a few blocks north of the church; neighbors battle crack houses just to the south. West of the church, a block of family-owned businesses withstands the advance of well-known retail outlets, while an affluent neighborhood to the east points to the new Starbucks as a sign of progress. Some of the richest and poorest citizens live within blocks of the church and of one another. A well-established university and a seminary are no farther from the church than a struggling public school.

The traffic in and out of the church reflects these intersecting lives. On their way to a meeting in the basement, the police chief and deputy mayor walk past volunteers who later that night will be hosting homeless neighbors spending the night in the church. Neighbors eating in the soup kitchen often pass tuxedoed groomsmen on their way to a wedding in the sanctuary. On Sundays, a robed choir that may be singing gospel one week and *Gesangbuch* the next flank a racially diverse staff.

Recent new members include a former senior executive of an international corporation, a local school board member, a social worker, and a formerly homeless man now leading some of the church's neighborhood efforts. These diverse people are being welcomed into a community that itself exists at, and in, the intersections.

"The church of a thousand crosses," as one architect described the facility, has one recognizable and prominent cross throughout the building and on most of its literature. It is a cross with a bright red heart situated in its upper-left quadrant. The cross has come to signify not only the location of the church at this busy intersection but also its location — grounded in the heart of the gospel — at the intersections "where spiritual journeys meet," to borrow a phrase that the congregation uses to describe itself.

Patterning our lives in the life, death, and resurrection of Christ invites us to discover intersections that we often otherwise turn into false alternatives — youth and age, strength and weakness, joy and suffering, abundance and sacrifice, tragedy and hope, community and solitude, church and world. Churches that live in these intersections are likely to manifest a commitment to resurrecting excellence precisely by being shaped by the gospel of Jesus Christ. In this chapter we focus on several crucial intersections and the ways in which gifted pastoral leaders continually help to cultivate their rich interconnections in faithful Christian communities.

The Letter to the Ephesians describes resurrecting excellence in ministry in this way: "I pray," the author writes to the church at Ephesus, "that you may have the power to comprehend, with all the saints, what is the breadth and length and height and depth, and to know the love of Christ that surpasses knowledge, so that you may be filled with all the fullness of God" (3:18-19).

We cannot see the whole scope of Christian life — the breadth and length and height and depth of it. We cannot assess fully its outcomes. The standard of excellence against which we measure our lives, the glory of God revealed in Jesus Christ, stretches out to infinity in every direction. We will never comprehend it entirely. It is the work of a lifetime even to try to bear a faithful witness.

But we can see the shape of resurrecting excellence at the point where breadth and length and height and depth meet. It is the shape of the cross — "the intersection," as Simone Weil once put it, "between creation and Creator."[1] There is no practice of Christian life that does not mirror that intersection. As congregants sing together, they live in the reality that last week's songs of joy intersect with this week's laments which they sing for those whose voice is robbed by

---

1. Simone Weil, "The Love of God and Affliction," in *On Science, Necessity, and the Love of God* (New York: Oxford University Press, 1968), p. 183.

tragedy. A group of parishioners visiting the home of a dying member will — on the same day — cross town to celebrate a young mother giving birth to her first child. From the four corners of the city, Christians will gather to pray at the scene of a recent murder, then gather at a neighbor's home to share food and dreams of a more peaceful week.

Clergy understand these intersections well. Every time a pastor reaches across the boundaries of the self to be truly present to another, every time she coaxes a word for her community from the strange, old words of Scripture, every time he leads his community into the worship of a God they cannot see and helps them feel God's claim on their lives, every time she washes a child or an adult in the waters of baptism, every time he sets the communion table and gathers the community from the north and the south and the east and the west, the intersection between creation and Creator is illumined.

Resurrecting excellence in ministry happens in intersections, and the pastoral leader is not simply a crossing guard. The pastor is an artist of the intersection, seeking connections among the often paradoxical dimensions of life — ancient texts and current dilemmas, inner experience and public responsibility, what has been and what yet might be. Gregory the Great once described pastoral ministry as the "art of arts," because the pastor seeks to heal the wounds of the human soul.[2] All of life is her business, whether it is manifest or hidden, public or private, external or interior. Gregory insists that the art of arts must be practiced at intersections. If you are drawn to contemplative prayer, Gregory would want you also to get out into the streets and care for the poor. If you are wholly absorbed in ministry with your neighbor, Gregory would want you also to spend significant time in prayer. It is the work of Gregory's pastor not only to move between the mystery of human life and the living presence of God but to live and work and pray and study and risk yourself at the places where human lives and God's life intersect.

The minister encourages the interruptions such intersections create. We can see this in its most crystallized form, perhaps, in the sacraments of Christian community, most especially baptism and Eucharist. Baptism continually interrupts the community by bringing new mem-

2. Gregory the Great, *Pastoral Care*, trans. Henry Davis, S.J. (New York: Newman, 1950), 1.1, p. 21.

bers into the body of Christ, longtime Christians intersecting with new ones. In the Lord's Supper, we are gathered "from the east and from the west, from the north and from the south" (Ps. 107:3) to the table where all of these directions intersect, a table where all are welcome, a table where the rich and the poor, the healthy and the sick, the whole and the wounded, the young and the old all drink from the same cup and share the same bread. Baptism and Eucharist ensure that Christian community is never static. They mark the essential intersections in Christian life, between God and humanity, self and other, community and world — intersections that reflect not only the shape of the cross but also the life of the one who died on it and then lived again. Pastors who know how to inhabit such intersections with courage and to invite their communities into them as well practice a resurrecting excellence, an excellence that is continually open to the movements of God's Holy Spirit. We now turn to stand at a few of those intersections.

Youth and Age

Communities shaped by resurrecting excellence can at once be in solidarity with those on the margins while boldly offering counsel to community leaders. They work to rear faithful children, while respecting and caring for elders. Where else are multiple generations being drawn together for an abundant life in the presence of God?

The first thing you notice in the photo is the man on the left, who is either giving the grinning teenage boy a hug or preparing him for a headlock. Several of the girls lean comfortably — one somber adult stare suggests *too* comfortably — against the communion table. Formality has given way to loosened ties and a pair of shoeless feet. Mostly there are glimpses and gestures of friendship and affection. Still, this snapshot of the 1988 confirmation class at Southport Church, with its rambunctious teenagers and slightly befuddled adults mingling around the communion table, hardly seems a recruitment poster for excellence in ministry.

In the mid-1980s, the leadership of this vibrant suburban church faced a familiar reality. Poor teaching on the part of the church and the competing claims of society had turned confirmation class into an agonizing experience for young people, their families, and their teachers. There were plenty of confirmation-age students. They simply didn't want to attend a Sunday afternoon lecture that reminded them of the very worst classes they encountered during the school week. Many parents were reluctant to push their children into something that might eliminate any connection to the church.

The new associate pastor — into whose lap the confirmation responsibilities were quickly unloaded — suggested to the education council a mentoring process that would match young people with adult members of the congregation. A new curriculum would include Bible study, worship, service, and prayer. But mostly, the program would encourage confirmands and their mentors to get acquainted, learn one another's stories, and together explore the questions and traditions of the faith.

The pastor asked parents to submit names of persons in the congregation whose lives were worthy of imitation. He asked confirmands which adults in the congregation they felt were good role models. The pastor quickly heard from those adults invited to participate. They were flattered, surprised, reluctant, and anxious. "I don't know enough about the Bible," was a common response, along with, "Are you sure I have anything to teach?" Still, nearly every adult who was asked to serve as a mentor agreed.

At the first gathering, the parents and mentors met separately from the confirmands. "Mentors are not surrogate parents," the pastor explained. "Most of us have learned how to live a Christian life by watching others. We hope the confirmands will find in all of you a worthy example. We think you'll also discover in them a relationship that strengthens your faith and practice." For their part, the confirmands expressed relief that they wouldn't be required to sit through "boring lectures" on Sunday afternoons.

The pastor encouraged the mentor-confirmand pairs to meet at least once a week, attend worship together, and participate in occasional gatherings of all the group members. The first official event was a weekend retreat at a nearby camp. In a setting removed from daily distractions, they would become acquainted with one another, build trust, and learn about the program. During the ride to the camp, the sounds on the bus alternated between teenage shrieking and stone silence. As they got off the bus and headed to their cabins, someone whispered in the pastor's ear, "Can I go home now?"

College students were on hand to lead the group through a series of rope courses and trust-building exercises. No participant was too old, too slow, too small, too big, too uncoordinated to finish. No one was ever on his or her own. Their goal was to finish as a group, unharmed but not unchallenged. Victory was declared only as the last person, not the first, crossed the finish line.

Living together is complicated enough in familiar settings, but the complexities are magnified in a strange place, where the people come from different homes and different generations, and measure success and happiness by different standards. All of this quickly became apparent, but was not hastily judged. The shoots of new relationships emerged in small gestures: of picking up a dishtowel and listening as the dishwasher told of his parents' divorce; of slowing one's pace to walk alongside an elderly friend.

Following the Sunday morning service of covenant and communion, even the sleep-deprived adults claimed to feel refreshed. Singing together was not their strong suit, but the group was beginning to find its voice. As group members boarded the bus, the change in attitudes and affections was palpable. Then, as the final bags were being stowed away, the head count revealed that three young men, who had been given permission to take a brief hike, were missing.

The reactions within the group ranged from "leave 'em behind and teach 'em a lesson" to "form a search party" to "let's hold hands and pray for them." The pastor reports that when the prodigals returned to camp ninety minutes after the scheduled departure time, their peers were at once more vocal in expressing their irritation and more forgiving than he could bring himself to be.

For over three months the confirmands and mentors were a visible and active presence in the congregation. Seventy-year-old Bob did not have grandchildren close by. His confirmand, the prodigal Andy, didn't have a living grandfather. Every week Bob and his wife would pick up Andy and go out for dinner and conversation together. "I don't know we learned that much Scripture tonight," Bob would tell Andy's parents when returning home. But Andy's parents could tell there was a growing affection and trust. Andy and Bob sat together in worship and participated in special events and work projects. They introduced each other as "my friend."

Mentors became a part of the confirmands' larger life, attending ballgames, concerts, family dinners, recitals, science fairs. As one young basketball player later commented, "It was kind of like having the church in the bleachers to cheer you on." Occasionally, several mentors and confirmands would meet together for Bible study, a work project, or to attend a wedding or funeral.

Not every pairing was a success. Some relationships were cordial but distant. A few were perpetually strained because the mentors lacked the time or the confirmands lacked the encouragement of parents. One relationship nearly dissolved because a confirmand ambitiously challenged his mentor at every turn. But in most cases the pairings worked.

Mentors and confirmands increasingly understood how their lives intersected with one another and with the church. Parents spoke appreciatively of the added support of another adult, and some faced up to their own need for support, encouragement, and deeper formation. The experiences offered different perspectives, sometimes even a new language for talking about the congregation's life together.

It would be nice to report that fifteen years later mentors and confirmands have remained friends and have grown more faithful and loving in their service to the church and in their life with God. In fact, many have. It would be wonderful to say that every young life has turned out just fine, but there have been unexpected pregnancies, drug abuse, family traumas, and estrangement. Some have wandered away, just like at that first weekend retreat. Some families have moved away; others have left to join another church; some are still wandering. A recent conversation revealed that many of the original group can account for nearly everyone else:

"She's had drug problems but is back and getting it together."
"He was in jail for a while but seems to have settled down."
"She's a nurse; we still get together once in a while."

One of the mentors reported a recent encounter with the parents of his former confirmand, who told him, "Our son's a youth pastor now, you know. He credits you and that confirmation class with shaping his call to ministry." The mentor could remember only a shy boy and awkward conversations. He was pleased but surprised that his young friend's life had taken on this new direction.

One story more than any other stands out in the memories of this confirmation class. Andy, who wandered off from the group at their first retreat, would leave them again. A rare cancer forced his early good-bye. Among the many friends and family who supported his last journey was his mentor, Bob. Unfortunately, soon after Andy was diagnosed, a fast-growing cancer lodged in Bob's back and moved up his spine. Bob and Andy were friends again on a new and final journey.

Bob's cancer progressed quickly. He told others he had experienced a good life and only wished he could be the one to die instead of Andy. The two of them visited, cheered each other on, and promised to see each other again. Nine months after Bob's death, Andy's memorial service was held in the same sanctuary where he had been confirmed five years earlier. "As in baptism Andy put on Christ," the pastor began, "so in Christ may Andy be clothed in glory." At open microphones, some of the mentors and confirmands spoke of Andy's friendship, laughter, crazy antics . . . and getting lost on the retreat. Even through tear-filled eyes, there was a clear picture of who these confirmands and mentors were and who they had become. And their voices sounded even better as they sang together with the whole church, and as the whole church sang for them.

Tragedy and Hope

In a consumeristic, individualistic culture, we are told, the generation weaned on television will be attracted to religion only if it is easy to swallow, entertaining, and fun. The danger of this approach to Christian life is that it runs the risk of obscuring the tragic dimension of human life, a dimension dramatically illumined by the cross. Whatever else it is, the story of the cross is a story of death, in which a teacher of great wisdom and compassion is executed by political powers in a form of exceptional cruelty. That it is also a story of resurrection and new life wrenched from death does not make the death itself any less tragic.

Resurrecting excellence in ministry calls us to work at the intersection of tragedy and hope, death and life, without diminishing tragedy's reality or obscuring the pain of death. Mabel Steele remembers the night her church was burned, a few days before the slayings of three civil rights workers. The burning of what is now Mt. Zion United Methodist Church occurred on June 16, 1964, and was one of sixty arsons in as many weeks at black churches in the South. In 2001, United Methodist Bishop Ken Carder asked Mrs. Steele, the only living member of Mt. Zion who was present on the night the church was burned, to return to the church and tell her story to members and guests of the bishop's cabinet.[3]

Bishop Carder had committed himself and his district superintendents to visiting the sites of pain and hope in Mississippi as an act of repentance and a movement toward racial reconciliation. The previous year, the United Methodist Church had announced its commitment to a national initiative of racial reconciliation. Bishop Carder believed repentance required blacks and whites of Mississippi to meet together in the particular contexts of their histories.

"We came to this church to have a business meeting," Mrs. Steele recalled of that tragic night. "We came in and had the meeting and then a car came up out in the yard. The people in that car were white men. All the people from the church went to their cars and trucks. My son, ten years old, turned out the lights."

The white men asked if the church members knew the whereabouts of the "white boys" — civil rights workers Andrew Goodman and Michael Schwerner, along with African American James Chaney. Later that night, the church was burned.

Clay Lee, a white pastor who in 1964 served the First United Methodist Church in rural Philadelphia, Mississippi, was also at the 2001 meeting. The morning after the burning, he had visited Mt. Zion to offer his congregation's help. An anonymous call that afternoon warned that if they followed through, "your church might be the next to burn." Lee, who became a United Methodist bishop in 1988, told the cabinet of the "code of silence" that gripped Philadelphia. "The light tried to shine in the midst of the ashes, and it got blown out time and time again," he said, and then sadly acknowledged, "I never knew if I did enough."

Four days after Mt. Zion's burning, the three civil rights workers were abducted and murdered. The discovery of their remains weeks later in an unfinished dam near Philadelphia drew nationwide attention to the FBI's efforts in the case, code-named MIBURN (Mississippi Burning). Nearly every year on the anniversary of the abduction,

---

3. We are grateful to Ken Carder for sharing this story with us.

national attention is again focused on Philadelphia, and the town's residents are reminded that this history has become their identity.

The Reverend Ed King, chaplain at Tugaloo College in Jackson and point person for Dr. Martin Luther King Jr., was also present when the United Methodists gathered at Mt. Zion in 2001. He told of threats on his life for his civil rights work. Rev. King played for the bishop's cabinet a recording of the eulogy he preached at the funeral of James Chaney. Within a year of that funeral service, Ed King was forced out of the Mississippi Annual Conference.

"I came in to this conference the year you had to leave," Superintendent Bert Felder told King. "I knew something of what was happening to you, but I didn't get involved. . . . I guess we all have our blind spots." Felder went on to talk about the "blind spots" in the life of white Christians in the 1960s, and just as he finished, Bishop Carder noticed a middle-aged black man slip into the back of the church. The man raised his hand to speak.

"We all have blind spots," the latecomer said. When I was growing up, there was a white pastor at First Church . . ."

Bishop Carder could feel his body tense. Was the speaker who seemed prepared to launch in on "blind spots" aware that the former pastor of First Church was present? The bishop looked at Clay Lee sitting in the front pew and sensed his discomfort. Bishop Lee's earlier concession had been an emotional moment, and Carder wished that this latecomer had been there to hear it.

". . . I was just ten years old when I heard that pastor on the radio. He said that it was wrong to spill innocent blood."

Bishop Lee had completely forgotten about that comment. In 1964, a group of clergy in Philadelphia decided they needed to make a statement about what had been happening. They appointed Lee to speak on the radio.

"White people and black folks all have blind spots," the speaker continued. "Mine was that I never had the chance to meet that man, and I should have thanked him."

After an expectant silence, Bishop Carder offered, "Well, now you have that chance. He's right here in the front row." Bishop Lee stood and met the man who as a ten-year-old boy had been touched by the words of "a white pastor" on the radio. The same boy who had turned out the lights the night Mt. Zion was burned — Arecia Steele, son of

Mabel Steele — was now a candidate for pastoral ministry in the United Methodist Church.

Outside the building near a marker honoring the memory of Chaney, Schwerner, and Goodman stands the church bell that sat in ashes in 1964. The site, Carder says, is "holy ground."

The excellence we see in such reconciliation is a reflection of God's patience, slowness to anger, and steadfast love. Shaped by the long view of God's steadfastness, we are called to remain faithfully and justly involved with our friends, clergy, and parishioners, our faith communities, and the world as we wait in hope for holy character to emerge.

Ministries of resurrecting excellence never forget the vulnerability and brokenness of human existence. Although rooted in the joy of the gospel and in gratitude for the many ways God sustains our lives, they are under no illusions about the damage human beings can do to one another or the capricious way that tragedy can strike a human life.

Annie Dillard advises writers to write as if they were addressing an audience of dying people. "What could you say to a dying person that would not enrage by its triviality?" she asks.[4] If this is a good question for writers, it is an even better question for ministers, as Richard Lischer discovered in the first parish he served. The former pastor of the church, dying of cancer, vested every Sunday and lay on a chaise lounge in the sacristy to listen to the sermon and participate in worship. "Whenever I stood in the pulpit during those first months," Lischer remembers, "Erich was a barely living blur to my right. If I was tempted, as preachers occasionally are, to replace the proclamation of the gospel with affable chatter, the presence of a liturgically vested, dying man in a chaise lounge never failed to dissuade."[5]

What can we say, what word can we speak to our brothers and sisters in this struggling world that does not enrage by its triviality? Such sensitivity does not mean that our Christian life should be dour. Nor does it mean that we should not sing for joy when we gather for worship: of course we should. What it means is that we are to work at the intersection of tragedy and hope without retreating to the corners

4. Annie Dillard, "Write Till You Drop," *New York Times*, May 28, 1989, Books section.

5. Richard Lischer, *Open Secrets* (New York: Random House, 2001), p. 66.

of either despair or false cheer. What it means is that we avoid like sin itself anything that trivializes our faith, anything that trivializes our vulnerable humanity, anything that trivializes the cross.

Simone Weil calls this cultivation of awe and wonder in the midst of sin and violence a sign of the desire to continue to love, to continue to turn oneself toward God in the midst of affliction, even when God appears to be absent. She calls it a sign of life. Sometimes, she says, it is possible to love only with "an infinitesimal part" of ourselves, but when we stop loving altogether, we are in hell.[6] It is love and hope in the midst of tragedy that keep us agile, that keep us able to bear witness to the justice God desires for all, that keep us from getting stuck in the hell of despair and defeat. It is the intersection of tragedy and hope that makes the shape of the cross visible in ministry. Ministry whose excellence can be measured by the breadth and length and height and depth of God's love combines a vulnerability to human tragedy and a deep and persistent hope that enables resistance to evil and celebration of grace and new life.

Strength and Weakness

A body spread out on a cross is utterly undefended, completely unable to ward off blows or protect itself in any way. A body spread out on a cross cannot even hasten its own death. The only thing such a body can control is its voice. All it can do is cry out: "My God, my God, why have you forsaken me?"

That new life was birthed from such utter vulnerability, such awful dying, is the central mystery of Christian faith. For Christians, the story of the death of Jesus on the cross is a story of strength drawn from weakness, power from vulnerability, life from death.

The Apostle Paul's ministry drew its themes from this paradox. Thrown to the ground and blinded, he received his call to ministry; imprisoned, he claimed freedom; a "fool for Christ," he proclaimed God's wisdom. Writing to the church at Corinth, he noted that few of them were educated or powerful or born to wealth. "But God chose what is foolish in the world to shame the wise; God chose what is

6. Weil, "Love of God and Affliction," p. 172.

weak in the world to shame the strong; God chose what is low and despised in the world, things that are not, to reduce to nothing things that are" (1 Cor. 1:27-28).

Christians in all times and places, particularly those without access to the kind of power and authority recognized by the world, have drawn on the paradox of strength in weakness to create ministries of resurrecting excellence. In the twelfth century, the visionary, poet, and preacher Hildegard of Bingen argued that the same "airy" temperament that left her vulnerable to illness and bodily weakness also blessed her with an increased vulnerability to the Holy Spirit.[7] Similarly, a woman named May, whose autobiographical account of enslaved life in the American South is preserved in the collection *God Struck Me Dead,* drew upon Paul's intersection of strength and weakness to interpret and undergird her call to ministry: "[God] has taken me, a fool — for sometimes my head was beat so I thought I was foolish — and hidden with me the secret of eternal life. He has made me to stand up on my feet and teach the world-wise out of his wisdom that comes from on high."[8]

Without the intersection of strength and weakness that marks resurrecting excellence, how would these women have answered God's call? The traditional paths to pastoral leadership were closed to them. They could not study in a seminary or "read divinity" with an established pastor. Neither would describe herself as literate. Hildegard had experienced chronic debilitating illness since childhood, and May had been beaten repeatedly by her owners. And yet their voices rise up out of the intersection of strength and weakness to reach us today, and their words and witness help shape the vocations of others who have been called by God to discipleship as well as pastoral leadership.

This dimension of resurrecting excellence runs counter to notions of excellence that rely on strength, efficiency, and influence. Christian understandings of excellence must always have at their heart a strong awareness of human frailty, brokenness, and even sin. Speaking of the Christian call to spread "the fragrance that comes from knowing

---

7. Hildegard of Bingen, *Liber divinorum operum* 3.10.38; PL 197:1038A.

8. May, "Slavery Was Hell without Fires," in *God Struck Me Dead,* ed. Clifton H. Johnson (Cleveland: Pilgrim, 1993), p. 156.

[God]," Paul writes, "Who is sufficient for these things?" (2 Cor. 2:14, 16). Who indeed? None of us is sufficient for the ministry of reconciliation to which we are called, none of us sufficient to relieve the suffering of the sick, the poor, the lonely, and the violated, none of us sufficient on our own to communicate the breadth and length and height and depth of God's love. Resurrecting excellence does not depend on moral perfection, workaholic behavior, or individual effectiveness. It depends on the intersection of human creativity with divine creativity and on communities of people who join together in a journey of faithfulness to God's inbreaking kingdom.

Because resurrecting excellence is rooted in the paradox of strength in weakness, it is necessarily communal in nature, as Paul knew when he developed the image of the body of Christ. There are many gifts, he writes, but one Spirit. There are many members of one body, and all are necessary for the body to function. Furthermore, "if one member suffers, all suffer together with it; if one member is honored, all rejoice together with it" (1 Cor. 12:26). Such a communal understanding of excellence requires the cultivation of friendship instead of competition. It focuses on the life of the community instead of individual achievement alone. It reflects the willingness to share in the burdens and joys of others instead of measuring them by their skills and productivity.

Christine Pohl reminded our colloquium group of just how difficult we often find it to maintain that inclusive, communal focus: "In an airport coffee shop a couple of years ago, I had a fascinating yet troubling conversation with a graduate student in liturgy. She was completely absorbed by the beauty, history, and mystery of the liturgy. Its practice and its study filled her life with joy. But then, in a passing comment, she said that she could not bear to participate in the liturgy of the church when it wasn't done well. For her, excellence meant a flawless and beautiful performance." Pohl confessed that she too has found herself at times "longing for, if not excellence, at least a more carefully shaped worship service." On one such Sunday, "a young girl with devastating disabilities was wheeled forward to participate as an acolyte in lighting the candles at the opening of the service. It was a slightly awkward moment, and a little distracting, but as she was returned to her place in the congregation, her eyes were shining with joy. We all sensed that something quite beautiful had just occurred."

Reflecting on the power of that witness to resurrecting excellence, Pohl concluded: "Somehow . . . , there has to be room for her brokenness and the gifts she brings to the community. There have to be congregations willing to acknowledge the mysterious connections between the cross and their healing, between brokenness and the goodness of their life together. Excellent ministry must ultimately draw us nearer to the brokenness of the cross as it simultaneously draws us to holiness and wholeness."[9]

In contemporary discussions of excellence, we are encouraged to "identify our strengths," "work from our strengths," "build on our strengths." And indeed, using our strengths for the greater good is an important dimension of being a member of the body of Christ. But in Christian life, we cannot work only from our strengths. We must constantly seek to find that place where our weakness intersects with strength — God's strength as well as the strength of the community. If our strength is pastoral care with the grieving, we must also be able to work with the congregation to create a budget that will allow the strengths of all to be engaged. If our strength lies in the struggle for social justice, we must also be able to respond to the person who wants to learn how to pray. If the strength of our community is lively and engaging worship, we must also be able to respond to the homeless men and women who gather on the church steps each evening. If our strength is in working with those who are already members of the church, we must also be able to reach out evangelistically to those beyond and outside the church. Resurrecting excellence calls us to work outside the boundaries of our strengths and interests, to cultivate the whole of who we might become by the power of the Holy Spirit.

Gregory the Great knew about the intersection of strength and weakness. He entered into the office of pope reluctantly, with tears, for he had been deeply content as the abbot of a monastery, living a contemplative life. With trepidation, he took on the new position to which he had been called, knowing that the power it afforded and the adoration he received from others could easily lead to self-deception. He tried to live as the "servant of the servants of God," but even in that he worried about how humility could obscure false pride.

9. Christine Pohl, "Reflections on Excellent Ministry" (Colloquium on Excellence in Ministry, Duke Divinity School, Durham, N.C., September 27-28, 2001), pp. 4-5.

Gregory knew that our virtues often mask our vices, that our strengths can obscure our weaknesses, even from our own view. "For the mind often lies to itself about itself," he writes, "and makes believe that it loves the good work, when actually it does not, and that it does not wish for mundane glory, when, in fact, it does."[10] Gregory urges the pastor not to believe his or her own press, not to be "diverted by the commendations of others," but to be vigilant in cultivating discernment, self-knowledge, and inner judgment. This is surely necessary for Christian communities as well as for ministers. Communities, too, have a way of allowing the celebration of their good works to mask their weaknesses. This is one of the most important reasons for communities and leaders to be working always at the intersections of strength and weakness, stretching ourselves to cultivate capacities that do not come naturally to us, to push beyond our scores on the Myers-Briggs or our mission statements. When adults at Southport Church were asked to mentor teenagers drawing near to confirmation, many were afraid they were not up to the task. But nearly every adult who was asked to serve as a mentor agreed to take a risk, to stretch, to try. And from that risk, both teenagers and adults shaped a community in which the faith of all was challenged and deepened. In ministries of resurrecting excellence, weaknesses are not hidden or repressed; rather, they are risked in intersections where they might be taken up and transformed.

Community and Solitude

Wise pastoral leaders encourage and equip their congregations for *koinonia,* or fellowship, so that ministry is ultimately seen as the work of the people and not of any particular person. If Mississippi's Bishop Carder had not been willing to work with a variety of people, the racial reconciliation he dreamed of would have had no chance to take root. If he had understood his task as the crusade of an individual, he would never have moved from town to town, inviting churches to move with him into the intersection of tragedy and hope and work for reconciliation that might be real and lasting.

And yet, excellent ministry also requires time apart. Jesus fre-

---

10. Gregory the Great, *Pastoral Care* 1.9, p. 36.

quently sought solitude in preparation for and in response to his interaction with others. Before he chose the Twelve, he spent the night alone in the desert hills. When he learned of the death of John the Baptist, he withdrew to a lonely place. Once, he attempted to retreat but ended up with five thousand dinner guests. Jesus frequently instructed his disciples to withdraw and pray. It was in the silence of a lonely mountain that Jesus' transfiguration occurred, and in the solitude of a garden that he prepared for his highest call.

For many pastoral leaders, however, desert hills and quiet gardens exist only in far-off dreams of sabbaticals or retirement. The "work to be done" occupies any corner of time or space that might have been claimed for periods of solitude. Yet we cannot pursue the richness of solitude only in intermittent rests from our work. When we do that, Sabbath is less a source of renewal than simply a well-deserved day off. Rather, we need the regular rhythms of Christian life that enable us to experience each week, and even each day, as marked by rhythms of work and rest, time together and time apart. Dietrich Bonhoeffer's classic book on the shape of Christian community, *Life Together,* is divided into two parts: the day with others and the day alone. But these are not two separate days; they are two distinct ways of receiving the gift of each day.[11]

Wise pastoral leaders understand that solitude is an antidote for, and not a cause of, loneliness. Solitude arises from divine silence. It is a response to the divine command, "Be still, and know that I am God!" (Ps. 46:10). In that silence, we begin to discern the otherwise indiscernible call of God and character of the community. Kyle Childress helped our colloquium understand the significance of this point. He noted that "a key to having an excellent ministry over a long period of time is caring about the particulars of ministry and people without being overwhelmed by them. And that requires space."

He continues: "What I mean by the particulars of ministry and people is that however large or small a congregation we serve, sooner or later ministry is done personally. A couple sits down in your study for counsel that is about them in particular. When the congregation comes forward for Holy Communion, you serve them personally, of-

11. Dietrich Bonhoeffer, *Life Together,* trans. J. W. Doberstein (New York: Harper & Row, 1954). See also Dorothy Bass, *Receiving the Day* (San Francisco: Jossey-Bass, 2000).

ten by looking each person in the eye and calling them by name, 'Fred, my brother in Christ, this is the body of Christ broken for you . . .'. Even in preaching, as the manuscript is being prepared, faces of the congregation come to mind. When you stand in the pulpit you make eye contact with these same people you have been visiting, counseling, and praying with all week and you know of their cancer, their divorces, their sin, their brokenness, their exhaustion, as well as their dreams and hopes and joys."

The problem, though, is that it can become overwhelming. Childress emphasized that "it is not that we no longer care about the particularity of people's lives but that we have more particularity than we can handle." But, he wrote, Jesus embodied another Way: "Jesus found space on a mountain to pray and one result of his prayer life was the ability to minister to people in particular. And if it was important for Jesus, then how much more important it must be for us to find space for prayer, worship, and other things which allow us to minister over the long haul."[12]

As this example shows, we need silence and solitude in order to care about our community and the particularity of its members. In and through silence we also become attentive to God and to others in new ways, discovering the significance of listening that shapes patterns of redemptive speech and silence in our life with others in Christian community.[13]

The context of Psalm 46 indicates that the injunction to "be still" is directed to the whole community. The following verse says: "The LORD of hosts is with us. The God of Jacob is our refuge." We cultivate attentiveness in the silence of solitude, and we also discover that the whole community is being called to stillness. We are to be attentive to the voice of God, both alone and in the midst of people. Jesus went away by himself to a lonely place to pray; and he also prayed with his disciples. So we cultivate faithfulness in the intersections of speech and silence, community and solitude.

12. Kyle Childress, "Wide-Open Spaces: Resources for Ministry over the Long Haul" (Colloquium on Excellence in Ministry, Duke Divinity School, Durham, N.C., September 27-28, 2001), pp. 1-2.

13. See L. Gregory Jones, *Embodying Forgiveness* (Grand Rapids: Eerdmans, 1995), especially chapter 6, for further discussion of the importance of redemptive speech and silence.

Church and World

Holy Family Lutheran Church resembles a rural congregation in that aging members have remained while younger members have moved toward the city — even as the once-distant city has moved in on the parish boundaries. Thus it shares with suburban congregations the familiar landmarks now emerging at its doorstep: coffeehouses, chain retailers, and upscale grocery stores. And like a center-city congregation, Holy Family has witnessed a gentrification it couldn't have imagined ten years earlier. But Holy Family defies the sociologist's description of rural, suburban, or center-city. The congregation occupies a plot of land near the Cabrini-Green housing project on Chicago's near north side — one of the nation's most notorious public housing developments.

Once regarded as an enclave of poverty, gangs, violence, and drugs, Cabrini-Green had been carelessly managed and shamefully ignored for decades. Reports of children sleeping at night in bathtubs for protection from drive-by shootings became national news. Jane Byrne, when she was mayor of Chicago in the early 1980s, made headlines by keeping an apartment in Cabrini in an effort to restore calm and safety.

By the 1990s, many of the densely populated high-rise buildings were torn down, and residents were dispersed throughout the metropolitan area. Today, Cabrini-Green is in the path of rapid gentrification, and the once-scorned real estate is prized by investors eager to develop property just a short train ride from downtown Chicago. Throughout the changes, Holy Family has identified itself as "a safe haven and spiritual home for the 5000 residents of Cabrini-Green."

On Sunday mornings, senior pastor Charles Infelt and youth minister Leslie Hunter lead a dynamic worship service that blends high-church liturgy, inspired gospel music, and lively congregational responses. About one hundred familiar worshipers greet each other and their guests with warm embraces and words of welcome. There is an uncommon mix of black and white, young and old, poor and well-to-do parishioners. The movement and flow of the service at first appears casual and unscripted, but it doesn't take long to discover that the service is anchored in ancient traditions reinterpreted for this place and these people.

On one Sunday morning in 2003, the pastor began his sermon with a discussion of how technology is used in warfare. His reference to a war half a world away might have seemed odd for a congregation struggling with its own battles in the next block. But the worshipers smiled and nodded attentively, urging the preacher on as the sermon moved between Iraq and Isaiah, considering the mind of God and the mind of humans. Nodding to a woman in the third row, the preacher noted that the hands and minds that shaped the weapons of war had also shaped the medical technology that brought healing to her sister's ill husband.

The movement from Word to Table was effortless. The worshipers gathered as family but made room for others. They prayed for themselves and interceded for sisters and brothers in different places. They thanked God for what they had and seemed unashamed to ask for what they didn't: patience with each other, hope for their struggling friends and neighbors, enough love and mercy to get them through the week. When the nearly two-hour service ended, no one seemed to rush out. There were chores to do and family news to share.

Holy Family's resurrecting excellence is grounded in their unambiguous proclamation that they serve a crucified and risen Savior. Their refusal to abandon what seemed a deadly place is testimony to their faith in God's eschatological vision. They were a stabilizing and welcoming presence in the days of gang battles and housing mismanagement; they want to continue that hospitable presence as a new racial and economic community emerges.

Under the umbrella of the Holy Family Ministries Foundation, the church has formed a school, a youth mentoring program, Bible studies, and health care groups. It sponsors a remarkable "Boys in the Hood" ministry that gives young boys a chance to discover their gifts and use those gifts to strengthen their community. While these ministries may seem extraordinary, the members of Holy Family would say that we all live in places where faithful followers of Jesus Christ are called to welcome the poor and the marginalized to our tables and congregations.

*   *   *

Two years after first visiting Holy Family, we spoke with Pastor Infelt about what was taking place. The area around Cabrini-Green was gentrifying, and Holy Family was welcoming the renewal while making sure that these new neighbors did not overlook the hidden beauty that had long been present and cultivated by the members and neighbors of the congregation. An old fence surrounding the church that had been battered by years of abuse was scheduled to be replaced with a new, modern one — that is, until the furnace went out. Furnaces trump fences in wintry Chicago. Then, supported by the generosity of community volunteers, the congregation began landscaping their bare, litter-strewn grounds so there would be places to congregate and welcome new guests. They began to talk of replacing the bullet-pocked plastic windows with glass so the new neighbors could see in and the church members could look out. And they decided, in that spirit, that there would be no fence. As one newspaper columnist commented upon hearing the news, "No fence. No defense against the world now except faith and a new philosophy: Fences say, 'Stay out.' Churches should say, 'Come in.'"[14]

Pastoral ministries of resurrecting excellence cultivate communities attentive to the intersections whereby we see more clearly the presence of God in the world. They create communities that are forever being interrupted by the sacraments of baptism and Eucharist, communities that continually make room for others. They create communities undergirded by habits and practices that, over time, transform life.

Resurrecting excellence has one shape but infinitely multiple manifestations. It shines forth from the intersections discovered in the pattern of Christ's cross. It calls forth leaders who, rather than giving themselves away until they are spent and dry, aspire to a way of living that fills them and the communities they serve with "the fullness of God." It allows prayer and justice, learning and living to continually interrupt and deepen each other. It is the life of "a still more excellent way."

14. Mary Schmich, "Serenity Now Also Outside Church's Doors," *Chicago Tribune*, June 5, 2005, Metro section.

3 *Resurrecting Excellence in the Christian Vocation*

> *The wellspring of excellence in ministry is this: God, who creates this magnificent world and in Jesus Christ reconciles and renews all things, graciously invites us to share in Christ's ministry by being reconciled and becoming agents of reconciliation. Excellent ministry, then, is God's gift. . . .*[1]

Resurrecting excellence in Christian life and ministry finds its referent, standard, and source in the excellence of the Triune God. The horizon of God's excellence is the glory of the creation given to us by the Father, the redeeming and healing love manifested in the life, death, and resurrection of the Son, and the sustaining and transforming work of the Holy Spirit, who is ever conforming us to Christ and making all things new. We are called to participate in God's "still more excellent way" in lives that both bear witness to, and contribute to, the *telos* of God's creation.

Ken Carder has described excellence in the Christian vocation as "being a sign and instrument by which creation is healed, reconciliation is experienced, and justice is practiced."[2] What does it mean to be

1. Kenneth L. Carder, "Excellence: Burdensome Expectation or Gracious Gift?" Sustaining Pastoral Excellence (SPE) Web site, http://www.divinity.duke.edu/programs/spe/articles/200506/carder.html.
2. Kenneth L. Carder, "What Does God Have to Do with Excellence?" SPE Web site, http://www.divinity.duke.edu/programs/spe/articles/200505/20050427a.html.

a sign and instrument of the work of God? It means developing eyes to see and ears to hear the beauty and excellence of God's work in the world. It means developing dispositions and habits of feeling, thinking, and acting that faithfully reflect and represent the beauty and excellence of God in diverse settings, circumstances, and lives.

Our primary focus in this volume is on resurrecting excellence among pastoral leaders. Yet in order to cultivate such a focus, we need first to attend to resurrecting excellence in the discipleship of all followers of Christ. Indeed, we believe that one of the pathologies in contemporary ministry has been a tendency to understand the pastoral leader as primarily an "expert" charged with tasks that are essentially distinct from the vocations of the laity and the congregation as a whole.

By contrast, we emphasize that pastoral leadership is best understood by moving first from God to discipleship as a vocation lived among and with others, and only then to the tasks specific to those who are charged with leading and shaping Christian communities. In this chapter, then, we will focus on the Christian vocation, the life of discipleship that is the calling of all Christians. We begin with a discussion of Christian discipleship, and then turn to the importance of Christian practices in shaping our discipleship.

The largest portion of the chapter is devoted to the significance of holy friendships in Christian life and pastoral ministry. This is a topic that generated wonderful energy in the colloquium, and became one of the most important touchstones for our conversations. We became convinced that, while there are pitfalls to be avoided, holy friendships are crucial for shaping faithful Christian discipleship as well as in addressing problems such as the loneliness and isolation of pastoral leaders.

Christian Life as Discipleship

In the fourth century, St. Jerome described baptism as "the ordination of the laity." Our discipleship, our ministry, is in the first instance the vocation, enabled and empowered by the Holy Spirit, of living ever more deeply into our new life in Christ. Thus Christian ministry — for all Christians — bears witness to the light of Christ by the power of the Spirit as we journey toward the fullness of God's kingdom in the communion and fellowship of the church. In this life of discipleship, we learn to love God truly and faithfully through an ongoing process of calling, educating, and shaping.

The essential elements of this process — calling, educating, and shaping — are closely bound to the patterns of feeling, thinking, and acting that characterize the "mind" of Christ (*phronein*; see Phil. 2:5), as we discussed in Chapter 1. And indeed, we see them reflected in Jesus' exposition of the life of discipleship in the first part of the Great Commandment: we are to love the Lord our God with all our heart, and soul, and mind, and strength (see Mark 12:30). At times, we emphasize one element to the exclusion of another. We pour out our hearts, neglecting the gifts of mind and soul. Or we are mind-full, but heart-less. But it is only in the interrelations of heart, mind, and strength — of feeling, thinking, and acting; of being called, educated, and shaped — that we truly begin to bear witness to the Triune God's presence in, through, and for the sake of the world.

Responsiveness to the calling of Christian discipleship is rooted in a deep attentiveness to desire. We see this reflected in the writings of the early church — for example, Augustine's famous "Our hearts are restless until they rest in thee, O God," and Gregory of Nyssa's insight, from *The Life of Moses*: "This truly is the vision of God: never to be satisfied in the desire to see [God]. But one must always, by looking at what he can see, rekindle his desire to see more. Thus, no limit would interrupt growth in the ascent to God, since no limit to the Good can be found nor is the increasing of desire for the Good brought to an end because it is satisfied."[3]

These passages suggest that the ordering of desire is crucial to how we live in relation to God. Yet, as both Augustine and Gregory elsewhere describe — and Augustine, centrally, in relation to his own life! — our desire is typically disordered, such that even when our patterns of feeling, thinking, and acting are open to reform, unless our desire is simultaneously open as well, we will fail. As Paul tells the

---

3. The quotation from Augustine is found in the opening paragraph of his *Confessions*. See Augustine, *Confessions*, trans. Henry Chadwick (New York: Oxford University Press, 1991), 1.1.1, p. 3; Gregory of Nyssa, *The Life of Moses*, trans. Abraham J. Malherbe and Everett Ferguson (New York: Paulist, 1978), 2.239, p. 116.

Romans, the good we would do we frequently do not, and the evil we would otherwise avoid we end up doing (Rom. 7:14-20). Desire can be difficult to bring under control. That is why we need others to help educate us for discipleship.

The church is a school for discipleship, the central context in which we are educated to live as disciples who are learning to desire and love God truly and faithfully. Our vocation is typically lived in the world (and always for the sake of the world), but our schooling throughout life is found in the church.[4] It is no coincidence that our best hopes for, and deepest disappointments with, Christian life are connected to a particular people and particular place.

This helps explain why the excellence of pastors is inextricably related to the excellence in ministry of all Christians, especially in and through the community of the church. In our colloquium we often heard stories of excellent pastors and excellent congregations mutually supporting and encouraging one another. We also learned that excellent pastors can flourish for only so long in mediocre or destructive congregations, just as excellent congregations can remain so for only so long under mediocre or destructive leadership. Such imbalance inevitably disorders our life together.

The discipleship of Christian faith and life has significant analogies to mastering crafts such as music or athletics. Indeed, Scripture draws on both in describing Christian life — see, for examples, Revelation 14:3-5 for music, and 1 Corinthians 9:24-27 for athletics. Each requires distinct educative formation; further, each requires distinct shaping, through the cultivation — or "rehearsal," if you will — of particular habits and dispositions that allow its practice to become

---

4. In his justly famous and influential book *The Purpose of the Church and Its Ministry* (New York: Harper & Row, 1956), H. Richard Niebuhr suggests that the purpose of the church and its ministry is the increase of love of God and neighbor. There is much to commend this suggestion, grounded in the twofold Great Commandment and aptly pointing toward our responsibility to both God and neighbors near and far. However, such a suggestion needs to be unpacked, in ways that Niebuhr did not, to explore and explain how and why the church is so crucial for us appropriately to love God and neighbor, much less why it is crucial if we are to "increase" in that love over time. In short, we must encourage Christian communities to wrestle with the question of why the church, and especially congregations, matters — to God, to us, and to the contemporary contexts in which we live.

"second nature." Christian discipleship is distinguished, however, by a more comprehensive process than either music or athletics — in both scope and, to some extent, duration. It involves the whole of our lives, not just one particular gift or set of skills. It is a lifelong process of unlearning sin and learning holiness.

On this journey toward the fullness of God's kingdom, we are called to bear witness to the Holy Spirit's work of making all things new. For this, God's grace continually offers us strength, but in the present life, the journey never ends. The life of Christian discipleship is shaped by a destiny not yet fully revealed, a destiny for which we need to unlearn sin and learn holiness so that — to use a term particularly appealing to Gregory the Great, Augustine, Aquinas, and Teresa of Ávila, among others — our desire will be manifested in true and faithful "friendship with God."

Resurrecting excellence in the Christian vocation arises from a life of discipleship that is called, educated, and shaped in Paul's "more excellent way." Christians who are described as "knowing what to say" or "being in the right place at the right time" are likely people who remain attentive to God and holy Scripture, who cultivate wisdom and knowledge through careful study, and who engage regularly in Christian practices and friendships that open our eyes and ears to the presence of God in and for the world.

Resurrecting excellence is learned and lived in the company, and under the guidance, of other people in and through the communion and fellowship of the church. This company includes both those who have gone before us and those who are around us. We yearn for the wisdom that comes from those who have had eyes to see and ears to hear over the years. Most fundamentally this is shaped by the writers of, and characters whose lives are told in, Scripture, and the ways in which our lives are thus shaped by, and located in, the Word of God. We also find wisdom in our forebears, such as Gregory the Great, whose relationship with, and understanding of, God is a wellspring for our own discernment and faithfulness.

Such wisdom also involves attending to wise contemporaries. It involves the capacity to understand developments and challenges in our own time, whether that means drawing on people who have different expertise to help us understand particular issues, or whether it means engaging people from different perspectives who illumine our own blind spots. So, for example, Mary Oliver's gifts as a poet enable us to see the glories of God's good creation in fresh ways; Gustavo Gutiérrez's *On Job* illumines the central role of poverty and the plight of the poor in that book that we had always read as a philosophical treatise on evil; Billy Graham's evangelistic outreach focuses attention on the Great Commission; Alasdair MacIntyre has shown the significance of the virtues, practices, and practical reasoning for faithful living; Desmond Tutu writes about and embodies the life-giving character of forgiveness; Wendell Berry draws our attention to the need for, and promise of, sustainable agriculture; Pope John Paul II powerfully calls the world to bear witness to "a culture of life"; and Gardner C. Taylor exemplifies black church preaching that connects deep learning and social engagement in New York City.

One of the crucial ways in which we learn to discern our own particular Christian vocation is through study of influential scholars and practitioners who have gone before us as well as study of, and with, wise contemporaries. We hope this is cultivated in local congregations as a part of the ongoing education of people from young children to older adults. It is also a critically important task during times of discernment for youth and young adults. Offering opportunities for such reflection through church-related colleges and vibrant campus ministries is important for helping young people discern their vocation as disciples of Jesus Christ.

Christian Practices

The lifelong learning of discipleship involves our being immersed in Christian practices — formative activities that "Christian people do together over time in response to and in the light of God's active presence for the life of the world."[5] These include such activities as singing, praying, and learning Scripture and doctrine — staples of our gathered life — as well as hospitality, forgiveness, and creating and caring for institutions.

5. This is the definition provided by the group that developed the book *Practicing Our Faith*, edited by Dorothy Bass (San Francisco: Jossey-Bass, 1997). The definition is found in the chapter authored by Craig Dykstra and Dorothy Bass, "Times of Yearning, Practices of Faith," p. 5.

These practices are important in several ways. First, they open us up to receiving the gift of God's grace, to seeing the power of the resurrection for cultivating new life in the Spirit. So, for example, for the disciples on the road to Emmaus, the practice of hospitality in the breaking of the bread opened their eyes to see the risen Christ (Luke 24:13-35).

Further, we often discover in doing these things that we are actually the recipients of something far greater than we have done — we receive new eyes to see the abundance of God's grace, new ears to behold the beauty and excellence of God's word. The effect on the church, as Nancy Rich observed in our colloquium, is profound: "The transformation that takes place through this encounter with the power and presence of the living God changes the church from the consumer mentality which asks, 'How much can I get (for how little I give)?' to 'How much can I give for all I have received?'"[6]

Practices and vision are thus inextricably linked, each offering rich generative potential for the other. This interplay was evident to our colloquium in Michael Brown's narrative of the life of a small Indiana congregation. Located in a predominantly white area near a university campus, this African American church seemed to have little potential for growth. Yet encouraged by Brown to discern and articulate a vision for their purpose and mission within the community, the congregation embraced the Apostle Paul's image in Philippians 3:14 of "pressing toward the mark." Not long thereafter, a mixed-race couple and their children began to visit. A sense of dis-ease was palpable among the congregation. People were uncomfortable with the prospect of such a family being a part of the church. Yet Brown welcomed them, even as longtime members privately expressed discomfort with their presence.

Over time, the church's commitment to hospitality pressed them to see things in fresh ways. Brown encouraged them to adopt an image of God as "colorful" rather than "colorless." Eventually, the congregation embraced the family. As a result, Brown reflects, "other mixed-race couples started to come. We continued to practice hospitality and embody communion. About a year after the initial couple's arrival, I looked out one Sunday morning and we were truly a diverse

6. Nancy Rich, reflection (Colloquium on Excellence in Ministry, Duke Divinity School, Durham, N.C., September 18-19, 2003), p. 1.

worshiping community. We were manifesting our vision of 'Pressing Toward the Mark.' Through practices our vision was becoming a reality. At that very moment, I realized how our vision contributed to the universal vision of God. Our words had become flesh."[7]

Particular practices of Christian life, such as hospitality, provide eyes to see and ears to hear God's way in the world. At the same time, they cultivate habits that help us unlearn sin and learn more faithful ways of living. Those practices and habits must themselves be dynamic, always open to the leading of the Holy Spirit, always open to correction and change. Lillian Daniel reminded our group of the intentionality with which that openness must be exercised.

> In my church, the Passing of the Peace moved from a frozen affair between two people to ten minutes of chaos in which people wandered the sanctuary greeting others. A new member confessed that it was actually his loneliest moment in the entire service. As others warmly greeted those they already knew, his few stiff greetings left him aware that he was not yet included.
>
> After that, we talked as a church about how the Passing of the Peace was not the time to socialize but to offer Christ's peace, and that Christ would call us to search out the newcomer. We had to pull ourselves back to a theological understanding of sharing peace, lest we forget our purpose and slide into simply worshiping ourselves and one another.[8]

On another occasion, Daniel began to feel that her congregation's disinterest in, and perhaps vague suspicion of, the unfamiliar practice of testimony was limiting their experience of worship. Conscious of the members' sensitivities yet convinced of their hunger for deeper participation, Daniel and the lay leaders of the church introduced the practice gently, as simply "reflections." "In the end," Daniel told our group, "the congregation was transformed."

7. Michael Joseph Brown, "Vision in Ministry" (Colloquium on Excellence in Ministry, Duke Divinity School, Durham, N.C., September 19-20, 2002), p. 9.

8. Lillian Daniel, "The Rough Edges of Holy Friendship" (Colloquium on Excellence in Ministry, Duke Divinity School, Durham, N.C., May 16-17, 2002), p. 11; available on the Sustaining Pastoral Excellence (SPE) Web site, http://www.divinity.duke.edu/programs/spe/articles/200506/daniel-p1.html.

Ministry flourished, but in the small delicate way it does in real churches. There was no apocalyptic fanfare, just the opening of hearts through the hearing and telling of God's story in worship, that ordinary little intersection between the way of life and the way of death. . . .

Without using the traditional words, these Christians were reflecting on where they had seen God in the practices of the faith. From what I heard in their words, in each case, it was the practices of the faith that had opened their eyes. One practice leads to another.[9]

Faithful, dynamic practices and habits beget others, practice unfolding into practice as we live into our life together.

We are increasingly convinced that *careful attention* to practices — and to the diverse crafts that contribute to a practice — is indispensable to cultivating genuine excellence. An essay by Daniel F. Chambliss, "The Mundanity of Excellence," focuses on the differences between Olympic swimmers and others who get close to Olympic level. He concludes that it is not so much talent or hard work as it is a willingness to focus attention on the mundane that is most central to fostering excellence. Chambliss notes: "Of course there is no secret; there is only the doing of all those little things, each one done correctly, time and again, until excellence in every detail becomes a firmly ingrained habit, an ordinary part of one's everyday life."[10]

Might our receptivity to God's grace and love be shaped by our practiced commitment to the daily habits of Christian living? We are

9. Lillian Daniel, reflection (Colloquium on Excellence in Ministry, Duke Divinity School, Durham, N.C., May 17-18, 2001), pp. 2, 3; a fuller form of this reflection appears in Lillian Daniel, *Tell It Like It Is: Reclaiming the Practice of Testimony* (Herndon, Va.: Alban, forthcoming).

10. Daniel F. Chambliss, "The Mundanity of Excellence," *Sociological Theory* 7 (Spring 1989): 85. The Olympic athlete offers a strong image of the practiced commitment we believe is essential to resurrecting excellence. At the same time, the peculiarly inclusive nature of Christian excellence accommodates a very different image as well, as Ken Carder reminded us: "When I think of an athletic image for Christian ministry, I think more of the Special Olympics. . . . There can be a difference in level of skill that entertains and even inspires; but the gifts that transform, really transform, often come in unimpressive packages and even 'less than average' persons" (personal communication, July 28, 2005).

enjoined to pray for our "daily" bread and told not to be anxious for tomorrow (Matt. 6:11, 34). Christian life is marked by tending to Christian practices, and more specifically the daily activities of worship, work, study, and community. As Kathleen Norris suggests, "It is a paradox of human life that in worship, as in human love, it is in the routine and the everyday that we find the possibilities for the greatest transformation."[11]

Moreover, when engaged with other people over time, Christian practices bind us together with our forebears as well as with others around us in Christian community. Reflecting on a week spent in spiritual retreat with the community of Taizé in France, Nancy Rich told the colloquium:

> I was struck by the simplicity of the worship, yet the power and presence of God was palpable. In spite of sitting on the floor with almost 4,000 people, there was an intimacy with God that I have rarely experienced even in smaller groups. . . .
>
> [One] thing that clearly struck me was the number of gen X and gen Y who came long distances to Taizé, almost as if on a pilgrimage. Yet there were no gimmicks. Instead, the singing was almost ancient in its use of Latin chants and simple prayers in many languages. I watched as they became silent and reverent as they approached the very nondescript chapel, out of respect and obedience to the signs in every language that said, "Silence." I watched scantily dressed young people place a shawl over their tank tops as they entered the sanctuary as a sign of the holy place that it is.[12]

As Dykstra and Bass note, "Enter a Christian practice, and you will find that you are part of a community that has been doing this thing for centuries — not doing it as well as it should, to be sure, but doing it steadily, in conscious continuity with stories of the Bible and in frequent conversation about how to do it better."[13] Christian practices join us into communities in which we learn from those before us, as well as those around us, how to nurture patterns of faithful Christian life.

11. Kathleen Norris, *The Quotidian Mysteries* (Mahwah, N.J.: Paulist Press, 1998), p. 82.

12. Rich, reflection, pp. 1-2.

13. Dykstra and Bass, "Times of Yearning, Practices of Faith," p. 7.

As our stories indicate, excellent pastoral leaders both participate in Christian practices and provide significant leadership in equipping laity to do so. Sometimes they do so by deepening practices that are already marks of a community, or by introducing a new way of doing it; at other times they do so by introducing new practices into the repertoire of a community; at still other times their focus is on inviting and welcoming new people into the community and cultivating their participation in practices of Christian living.

Yet we are also aware that, at times, pastoral leaders can become so focused on sustaining the practices and equipping the laity for the practices that they are insufficiently attentive to engaging in them. For example, leading worship is not necessarily the same thing as engaging in worship. Creating the structures to nurture faithful Bible study in small groups is not the same thing as participating in a group.

This is particularly important because one of our contemporary challenges is to nurture healthier physical, emotional, and spiritual lives for clergy. Living healthy lives is a challenge of Christian discipleship generally; but indications in the 2001 Pulpit & Pew national survey (as well as in other studies) suggest that the clergy, taken as a whole, are not nearly as healthy as they should be. There is no single cause of this lack of health, nor is there one single cure. But we are convinced that nurturing more faithful participation in Christian practices by pastoral leaders in their capacity as Christian disciples will have a beneficial impact on their physical, emotional, and spiritual health. To take but one example: pastoral leaders need to model the faithful rhythms of work, rest, and play intrinsic to the Christian practice of Sabbath-keeping. Doing so is not only important to their leadership of others; it is itself an exemplary sign of their leadership.[14]

Christian practices are intrinsic to shaping and sustaining faithful discipleship of Jesus Christ. In and through these practices, Christians are joined to others in ways that develop over time into holy friendships. Such friendships are crucially important in helping us discern the truth of our own lives. That is, resurrecting excellence involves learning to see and hear God in the company of particular people, holy

14. We are grateful to John Wimmer for the formulation of this point. He credits Roy Oswald for emphasizing that attending to the rhythms of Sabbath-keeping is an act of leadership.

friends, who help us unlearn sin and learn a more excellent way of living our lives in relation to God.

Holy Friendships

John Vincent founded the Urban Theology Unit in Sheffield, England, in the early 1970s. John devoted much of his life to strengthening the church and local community in a time and place that was economically impoverished and sharply divided along racial and ethnic lines. Shortly before his retirement, John was asked to describe his most significant contribution to the church and neighborhood. Rather than talking about economic development, membership growth, or ethnic understanding, John simply answered, "Alongside. I think we've made a difference by introducing the word 'alongside' into our life together. We've advanced from living apart to living alongside our neighbor."

As we listen to imaginative and faithful clergy and laity, they almost always describe ministry in terms of whom they have been alongside. They talk about how they have come to love congregants and pastors in spite of, and sometimes because of, their flaws. They describe ministries that are abundant because they bring together people who never imagined being alongside each other, let alone enjoying the relationship. They give testimony to how being alongside friends and strangers has deepened their awareness of how God is alongside them all. Their stories are irresistible even when they are tragic because they witness to a mutual encouragement that is more alluring than the rough individualism of the world and more beautiful than the seduction of sameness and homogeneity.

When we reflect on the call to discipleship, the life-giving character of excellent congregations, and the gifts of outstanding pastoral leaders, we are aware of the importance of the mutual encouragement and love that sustains people who learn how to accompany one another "alongside" us on our journeys. Communities of people are crucial to sustaining us through the joys and griefs of life, the triumphs and tragedies, the successes and failures, the fulfilling clarity and the perplexing struggles in discerning and living our vocations faithfully.

Indeed, having people who walk and work and live alongside us, people whom we call "holy friends," is indispensable to resurrecting excellence in Christian life. We all need holy friends in our own lives, and we are called to be holy friends to others. We are also called to show hospitality to strangers and to love our enemies, practices that help us discover the grace of navigating relationships in the light of God's friendship with the world, and with each of us, in Jesus Christ. In the midst of sin and brokenness, we discover through hospitality and searching love that strangers and even enemies can become holy friends in Christ.

There is no question that friendships — especially holy friendships — take time to cultivate and are often very fragile in their development. But these friendships also acquire beauty in the way that an heirloom acquires beauty with its scratches and nicks: evidence not that the relationship is abusive but that it is willing to risk the interruptions and demands that a gospel life encounters in every holy interaction. The congregation thus becomes critical to the shaping, correction, and celebration of these friendships. Like a healthy church dinner that involves more than food, holy friendships require more than people who are potential friends. These friendships are shaped, judged, celebrated, and held accountable within the movements, traditions, and structures of congregational life.

What, then, is distinctive about holy friendships and about the congregations in which these relationships emerge and are nurtured? How do we cultivate them, how do they help us interpret God's redemptive presence in our world, and what are the risks of becoming part of such an adventure?

Friendship with God

We have argued that Christian discipleship is fundamentally learned and lived in and through the practices of Christian communities. Christians "congregate" because of the character of the God we worship, because of our status as creatures created for communion both with God and with others, and because we yearn for particular relationships that can help nurture in us the capacity for living faithfully. We have suggested that we need holy friends, and we need to live as holy friends with others, if we are to overcome disordered desires, unlearn habits of sin, and learn how to live faithful and holy lives in relation to God.

Yet in contemporary America we often find Christian friendship difficult to understand, live, and even desire because of our dominant picture of ourselves as rugged, isolated individuals. Modern Western cultures have tended to emphasize, and at times even glorify, the individual. Individuals, so we are implicitly (and sometimes explicitly) told, need to resist collectives, those impersonal structures that seek conformity, impose rigidity, and stifle creativity and freedom of expression. This notion of the individual, especially as it is defined over against conformity, is descriptively false and normatively dangerous.

It is descriptively false because none of us becomes a person by separating our individual identities out from others. We might engage in such attempts as a part of adolescence, struggling to discern who we are apart from our parents and other social influences we outgrow at this stage. But maturity as adults calls us to discover the reality of our interconnectedness with others. This adolescent individualism, if left unchecked even as we grow older, is dangerous, because we deny the other people around us who provide challenge and support. Even more importantly, we fail to recognize that we can overcome our tendencies toward self-deception and other forms of sin only through deep and loving engagements with God and others.

We can find such engagements, but only if we renounce the individualistic picture for one that is more truthful to God and to the realities of our own lives. The God whom Christians worship is not a solitary God, far removed from the world in which we live. Rather, we worship the Triune God, who is characterized by self-giving love.[15] Further, God loves those whom God has created. God wills communion with creation and creates human beings in the divine image and likeness. We are created for loving communion with God, with one another, and with the whole creation. Hence, we can fulfill our destiny as human beings only when we fulfill our God-given capacity for loving communion. It is for this reason that we gather in congregations as Christians.

But there is a second, and more urgent, reason why we gather as Christians: we human beings have persistently failed, and continue to

15. For further exploration of this understanding of God, human life, and the realities of sin, see L. Gregory Jones, *Embodying Forgiveness* (Grand Rapids: Eerdmans, 1995).

fail, to live faithfully in love with one another. Our lives, and even our gatherings in communities, are marked persistently by the brokenness of sin. This brokenness, an underlying reality that mars human life, is manifested in a variety of ways — ranging from a self-focused pride that "I am at the center of the universe" to an equally self-focused despair that "I have no identity, no worth at all."

This always-already brokenness is the fundamental condition of sin. It is marked by human self-deception and our propensity for moral and spiritual blindness. This fundamental condition also manifests itself in particular and specific sins. Such sins include both things that we do *to* one another and things that we *fail* to do *for* one another. In either case, we not only diminish the other(s); we diminish ourselves.

We are not freed from this destructiveness by individualistic, consumeristic spirituality. Nor are we freed by human forms of congregating that replicate and often intensify the divisiveness and self-deception that mark our individual lives. Only the work of Christ, through his life, death, and resurrection, and the ongoing work of the Holy Spirit, redeems us from our sinful self-deception and frees us for new life — the life for which we were originally created. God in Christ "capacitates" us for the friendship for which we were created and by the Holy Spirit draws us into new relationships to sustain us and lead us to discover the life that really is life.

Yet, we might ask, how does this happen? Put differently, what gives individual humans, as well as whole communities, the capacities in our day-to-day lives to root out sin and to grow in our ability to attend to the Truth and live faithfully and responsibly? How do we learn to sustain life in the Spirit?

God's initial offering of holy friendship occurs for us at the edge of the baptismal waters. In the initiating rite of baptism, we become disciples of the One who personifies God's friendship for us. Baptism interrupts our way of forming friendships based on what we hope to get out of them. In our new life of discipleship we learn a language that defies conventional wisdom about friendships: stories that tell of welcoming the stranger, loving the enemy, and describing as family those for whom water is thicker than blood.

Introduction to the baptismal covenant and the baptized community ought to reflect the surprise, delight, and expectancy that we feel when we see a friend in the face of a stranger. God, in the life of our friend Jesus and in the companionship of the Holy Spirit, is introducing us to holy friends: congregants among us, saints around us, traditions, practices, and stories.

At every baptism, we renew our friendship with God and are reminded of all those who have been and will be invited to share in that friendship. We do not choose those God calls into community; rather, we are chosen and joined together in God's redemptive acts of salvation.

Brought Together by Providence, "Capacitated" by Grace

It is exhilarating to consider a vision for Christian life that is shaped by friendship with God, patterned in Christ, and seeking the benefit of others through holy friendships. Too often, however, that vision is not reflected in the reality of the church. We are not very practiced at articulating relationships that are deeper than mere association with like-minded people. Even those that do move a bit deeper into friendship are likely to arise out of common work, a shared task, a mutual joy or burden. "He's an old school friend," we say of the person we seldom see but who shares the stories and memories of past high school or college days. A deeper set of common interests and activities creates identities for our friends: she's my dance partner, or he's my traveling companion. As long as we share these activities or interests, the relationship is sustained. The risk, of course, is that it remains at these more superficial levels and leaves untouched our deepest joys and griefs, yearnings and hauntings, hopes and fears. Over time, the friendship diminishes, or even disappears.

Further, not every mutual attraction produces a healthy relationship. Some are destructive and corrupt. Cynicism, substance abuse, financial impropriety, and sexual indiscretion have launched many relationships that ended in tragedy and heartbreak for those involved and for their larger circle of friends and family. Supporting one another's sins and self-deceptions is hardly the basis for a life-giving friendship.

Indeed, all friendships need accountability. Even mutual affection for the gospel can become a misplaced admiration of our personal desires and self-interest. It is important to be alert to the corruption of the friendship and the community when attraction becomes infatuation, or when others are neglected. Holy friendships require accountability to Christ and to the practical wisdom of mature Christians who can speak plainly and truthfully about the shape of holy friendships as well as their distortions and corruptions.

Holy friendships relish an orientation beyond our personal preferences and appetites. Friendships we initiate are often controlled and manipulated to suit our desires or circumstances, but a holy friendship is initiated by God and brings God's ways to life. Holy friendships do not begin, or end, solely on our terms. They are shaped by God's grace in Christ, and we learn how to nurture them in and through the church.

Why do we call them "holy" friendships? We do so for two reasons. First, these relationships are often unlikely to be developed apart from a mutual attraction to the gospel life. They bring people together from different backgrounds and histories, with diverse hopes and fears. And, second, they are oriented toward discernment and deepening of Christian vocation, as well as nurturing growth in Christian life, toward our learning how to live as holy people. It is not that these friends must already be holy; indeed, given the shape of Christian life, that would be impossible. Holy friends are our companions on the journey of learning to desire and love God truly and faithfully.

How do holy friends shape us in our discernment, and in our growth? Holy friends are those who, over time, get to know us well enough that they can challenge sins we have come to love, affirm gifts we are afraid to claim, and dream dreams about how we can bear witness to God's kingdom that we otherwise would not have dreamed.

We do not need people to challenge sins we already hate; we are already clear about them. Nor do we need people to affirm gifts we have already claimed; it is nice to have our own awareness confirmed, but it is not news. We do need people who can help us discern where God is working in our lives, calling us to cast off those distorted and distorting sins that weigh us down, that have become so much a part of us that we can rationalize them away and pretend they are not even there. We also need people who can see where God's Spirit has been moving to encourage us, who can see signs of growth where we are prone to stay stuck in the familiar. And when these people help us dream dreams, they enable us to cast off that preoccupation with self that is a condition of sin and to cultivate eyes to see and ears to hear God's abundant grace and loving work in the world.

Clement and Robert are unlikely friends. Robert is a lawyer, public policy expert, and well-paid consultant to state government agencies. When he's not earning frequent-flier miles, he's listening to opera with his wife, attending his daughter's high school activities, or kibitzing with one of his many siblings about the care of an aging parent with dementia. Robert is generous, faithful, and, by nearly every measure, successful in his life and work.

Clement shined shoes for many years at a private downtown club. Before that, he washed windows. Since then he's tried to find work as a grocery bagger and teacher's aide but complains that "nobody wants to hire an old man without schoolin'." Widowed and estranged from his children, Clement lives in a cluttered apartment with his two birds, stacks of books, stuffed animals, and a few of his pencil drawings taped to the wall. He deflects challenges and condescension with one of two responses: "I'm not educated, but I've got street smarts" or "I'm a survivor."

The two men seem to have very little in common. They are separated by race, economic class, neighborhood, education, family background, and social status — all the things that typically account for how we become acquainted with one another. And yet, Clement and Robert meet regularly, talk on the phone nearly every Saturday, and weekly gather where their friendship began: at church. They agree that the church has become their school for an unlikely friendship.

Well-positioned in a safe and comfortable environment both at work and at home, Robert acknowledges that he spends much of his time either apart from, or flying over, the diverse contours of society. His yearning to walk the boundaries and margins of his community has led him to a variety of relationships. He has been the only white employee in a predominantly African American enterprise, one of the few male colleagues in an advocacy group made up of mostly women. When he met Clement in their middle-class, downtown congregation, Robert saw a kindred spirit. "I had the sense he was living on the edge of his own comfort zone by attending this church, and I wanted to get acquainted."

The early gestures of friendship were modest. They sometimes sat together at church and almost always chatted during the coffee hour following worship. Clement likes to tell the same four or five stories to whoever will listen. Rather than being put off by the repetition, however, Robert began to realize he was being invited to share in a life and world he didn't know. "There's a paucity of language in Clement's stories," Robert admits, "but there's also a genuine invitation to share life together."

Over time, the conversations at church led to an exchange of phone numbers, which led to Saturday morning telephone conversations. The textures and wrinkles of their life stories unfolded slowly, neither revealing more than he felt comfortable with or pressing the other into awkwardness. The occasional embarrassed silence or clumsy response signaled which doors were open and which were closed.

More than anything else, the economic disparities of their lives might have made for an uncomfortable if not disruptive obstacle in their relationship. The church they attend provides a Sunday meal for homeless and low-income neighbors. Robert and Clement have stood on opposite sides of the serving counter. Robert lives in a comfortable, well-kept suburban home. Clement lives in a rather untidy, federally subsidized apartment across from the church. They will occasionally take turns buying one another coffee when they get together but never go out to eat because, as Clement reminds his friend, "some of these places will charge you as much as $4.50 for a meal."

"I don't want to be his ticket," Robert acknowledges, "and he doesn't want to be my token." They exchange a different sort of currency. Although they will give each other a small gift once or twice a year — art supplies from Robert, a sketch or drawing from Clement — they mostly share their time, attentiveness, and stories. "I spend my working days in a professional culture that says people are fungible," Robert reflects, "but Clement and I can't just replace each other."

"Yeah," Clement adds, "because we're friends." When asked to explain what that means, Clement seems a bit put off. "He's not my sugar daddy. We trust each other. He takes me places, but I can take him places too." Clement pauses to think about what he has just said and laughs. "We've gone lots of places together."

It is unlikely that Clement and Robert would have met anywhere other than in their congregation; even less likely that they would have been able to sustain the relationship for nearly ten years without strong faith commitments and the nurture of their local church. Located in the heart of downtown, the church has remained in the same place for over 175 years. Its very presence says something about the importance of continuity and stability.

Robert and Clement also note the importance of worshiping together. Every service begins with the Passing of the Peace and ends with the congregation singing "Shalom to You." "The pastors of the church continually emphasize that it is God bringing us together," Robert reflects. "And when we come to the communion table, you can't help but look around and realize that only God would have brought *this* group of people together!"

We need the presence of others to keep us from self-deception, to remind us when our sins are masking as virtues or our tolerance is being used to isolate rather than welcome others. We need to share with others the common, restoring wealth of hymns and Scriptures, traditions and liturgies when we reach the limits of our patience, interests, and abilities. We need the waters of baptism flowing through our lives to interrupt our habit of self-selecting relationships. Only then does God meet us as friend and lead us to other, even more unlikely friendships that we never would have found on our own.

Making Room for the Stranger

We must be careful that the holy friendships we form within the church leave room for interruption by other persons and other ideas. The higher the level of certainty we have about who our friends are, the greater the risk that we have neglected the depth and breadth of God's friendship.

Scripture reminds us that God often comes to us as a stranger, as an unexpected one. So the letter to the Hebrews enjoins, "Do not neglect to show hospitality to strangers, for by doing that some have entertained angels without knowing it" (Heb. 13:2). Throughout his ministry, Jesus scandalized friends and enemies alike as he welcomed strangers and those estranged because of belief, nationality, income, or gender. "Day by day," we are reminded in the Acts of the Apostles, the early church was welcoming strangers and adding to their number those who were being saved (Acts 2:46-47).

Making room for the stranger will look and feel different depending on one's context. But such hospitality will always be communal, "alongside" those who are welcomed and those who offer the welcome. God's excellence is revealed when both guest and host share the gift of moving beyond politeness to attentiveness and the potential for friendship.

Mike Mather, formerly the pastor of Broadway Christian Parish in South Bend, Indiana, tells of a wintry Advent encounter in which strangers learned something of God's gift of friendship.[16] Because it was a snowy evening, there were only six members of the parish present for the service. When it came time to pray, there were loud sounds of teenagers at the side door. As people were reflecting on the Scripture reading in silence, Mike moved to the door and encountered a young teenager who wanted to know what was going on. When Mike told them about the evening prayers, the teenager asked if he and his friends could come in. "I considered that for a moment — I wasn't sure it would be a good idea. But of course I said, 'Sure.'"

The young man and his buddies came in and sat down. The group continued in silence for a short time and then moved into the hymn. The side door of the church opened again, and there were more young voices. "Are our friends here?" the young men asked. "Would you tell them to come out?"

Mike was firm. "No. But you're welcome to join them if you wish." The pastor acknowledges he was hoping just a bit that they might say no . . . but they didn't.

They came in and knelt down next to the first young man and whispered something in his ear. They were asking him to leave, but he stood his stead, and the others sat down, not particularly any happier than anyone else wondering what was about to take place.

Mike explained how prayer time worked: Anyone could offer a prayer. When a person finished the prayer, he or she would say, "Lord, in your mercy," and everyone else would say, "Hear our prayer." The prayer time began and the congregation was invited to join in. There was silence, then some chatter among the young people. Mike started to say something to them, but then a member of the congregation of-

16. Thanks to Pastor Mike Mather for sharing this story with us; a larger account of this incident is described in Mike Mather, *Vital Ministry in the Small Membership Church: Sharing Stories, Shaping Community* (Nashville: Discipleship Resources, 2002).

fered a prayer and concluded, "Lord in your mercy" and everyone responded, "Hear our prayer." The pastor acknowledges his eyes were wide open and focused on the young people.

The young people's eyes were wide open as well when they heard the congregation joining in. They began to add their own prayers. "For my cousin Booder, who was killed last year," one of them prayed and then hurriedly added, "Lord in your mercy" and everyone responded, "Hear our prayer."

Now all the young people were offering prayers for people in their families — many of whom had been killed. The teenagers were all noticeably eager to hear everyone joining them with "Hear our prayer." That night the gathering of friends and strangers prayed for the world, for places of violence, and for the schools. One of the young people prayed "that the schools would stop expellin' people!" and everyone said, "Hear our prayer." The time of prayer culminated when the young man who was the leader said, "For me and for my grandma, 'cuz my dad is tryin' to take me away from her." And everyone said together, "Hear our prayer."

Pastor Mike invited people to turn in the hymnal to the Lord's Prayer, and they prayed it together and then sang the hymn "I Want to Walk As a Child of the Light." The guests stayed and exchanged signs of peace along with the hosts. And then they left — much more quietly than they had come. A year and a half later when Broadway Parish was recognized for their work with young people, the pastor and congregation traced their efforts back to an openness in worship that snowy Advent evening.

Making room for the stranger usually requires a reshaping of life together. That reshaping may eventually manifest itself in cultural or organizational changes, but the welcoming often begins with gestures as simple as an open door or a shared prayer. Subtle movements and gestures sustain and strengthen the interaction among friends as well as strangers. Making room for the stranger is about discovering that our lives are inextricably connected with others.

A consumerist culture urges us to measure the costs of our involvement: What will I get out of this? Is this a good investment of my time? A cross-shaped community, however, trades in a different kind of economy. We do not make room for the stranger to have our needs met. We engage in these relationships because our needs already have been met in the friendship of God made known to us in the life, death, and resurrection of Jesus Christ. Because of this friendship, we are able to care for the needs of others. Often our needs are met — or more often, redefined — in these relationships, not as an orchestrated goal, but incidentally, and delightfully.

Bonds in the Midst of Brokenness

Following a sermon on forgiving one's enemies, a longtime member of the church lingered around the narthex. When others had left, she approached the pastor and asked in a calm but firm voice, "Do you really think I should forgive John?" John not only had left this woman who had been his wife, but he had maintained little contact with their children, and there was growing evidence that he had hidden a number of financial assets that should have been shared.

Sensing the personal pain and unease of his friend and parishioner, the pastor tried carefully to shape his answer. "I know it's hard. I know it doesn't sound fair. But hopefully you will be able, with God's help, to move toward forgiveness." He braced himself for what was sure to be legitimate rage at the idea.

"Good," she said without hesitation. "No one else among my family or friends believes that. I just need to know there is still one place that does."

For most of us, loving our enemies seems as preposterous as breathing underwater. When Jesus urges us to "love your enemies and pray for those who persecute you," we flinch at the idea that those who have suffered and been injured should be expected to forgive. We imagine situations where immense harm has been done — where brutal dictatorships have massacred citizens, where adults in responsible positions have exploited children. Not one of these experiences can be diminished or ignored. And yet, there are many people who search for some community to encourage them not only to find a way through the catastrophic experiences of life but also through the more ordinary encounters of betrayal and brokenness.

Sharing in God's more excellent way of loving our enemies begins with our acknowledgement that there are times and places we live as enemies and with enemies. In too many instances, we either deny the presence of an enemy or we label every disagreement as cause for naming and fighting a new one. Excellence is apparent in friends and enemies who can name the brokenness even when they cannot name the path toward reconciliation.

Lillian Daniel recalled for our group a moment at her denomination's annual gathering when delegates had been fighting about how the General President had been elected. "We had all heard his name dragged up and down the floor as if it were somehow disembodied from a real person, but now he stood before us ready to speak, with all the vulnerability of one who serves at the body's pleasure." The "enemy" — just about everyone was viewed that way by some other person or group — was not only named but made visible before the body.

The denominational official reminded the body that he belonged to Jesus Christ through his baptism. Daniel writes: "In that moment, he was clearly a pastoral leader but he was also delineating for us the limits of holy friendship. He understood that, whether he wanted it or not, he was now in a holy relationship with the delegates. . . . He was not able to choose these relationships, but he was able to determine their power over him."[17]

If all of our relationships — those of friends and strangers as well as enemies — are regarded as relationships not entirely of our choosing, then it becomes a matter of how we conduct ourselves in such relationships, including adversarial ones. In his pastoral memoir, *Open Secrets*, Richard Lischer describes a serious conflict he had with his lay leader, Leonard. A breach of trust, Lischer acknowledges, had festered too long and was much too obvious to the rest of the congregation. Each man was as stubborn in maintaining his position as he was in remaining committed to the ministry of the congregation.

When Lischer learned that a woman who lived near Leonard had overdosed on pills, he asked for Leonard's help, forgetting that they were not speaking to one another: "That was the beginning of the great thaw between Leonard and me. Our manner of reconciliation reminded me of the way my father and I communicated. . . . Always *through* something else: . . . throwing a ball, catching a fish, planting a tree, but never direct from one heart to another. We achieved approximations of feeling for one another, with the tacit understanding that the truth between

17. Daniel, "Rough Edges of Holy Friendship," p. 8.

people is cumulative. Everything will be sorted out at some mythical end point. Until then, extended conversation is premature at best."[18]

There are times to act swiftly and move boldly into the rough waters of our relationships. But often, quick movements cause churning waters to muddy further. Lurking under the surface are fears, emotions, and issues that are more likely to strike back than reach out. Likewise, struggling congregations may find that the remedy of a "fix" or a paid "fixer" is so disruptive as to bring simmering troubles to a full boil. Small gestures of affection and understanding, however, can rebuild trust.

Healthy relationships and congregations are filled with these approximations of greater peace and reconciliation. Flowers and food, embodying the larger gifts of beauty and nourishment, approximate the desire for healing and hope that can never be achieved with one sweeping act or movement. The exchange of peace, one of the most disarming as well as disconcerting activities for some worshipers, is God's tender movement toward us and God's gentle nudging of our lives toward others — and toward an understanding of a kingdom not yet fully revealed. To speak up when others are being silenced or to refuse to pile our opinions onto those already heavily burdened can be small steps toward a greater reconciliation.

We discover the power of patterning our lives in Christ as we learn how to nurture friendships, welcome strangers, and love enemies. These are sustaining relationships for our lives, leading us to respond to the gracious, overflowing love of Father, Son, and Holy Spirit by cultivating gracious and loving relationships.

Yet many of us spend our lives concealing and containing ourselves from others. This is a particular problem for clergy, who tend to inhabit the role of experts or professionals and thus see people as parishioners, or potential parishioners, but rarely as people with whom we can open up in vulnerability to the intimacy of friendship. We complain about living in a fishbowl, but we also feel safe in that glass enclosure. We allow ourselves to be seen, but we control when to touch or be touched, when to conceal our passions and emotions and when to reveal them. To make ourselves known to another is not to live without boundaries. But we need to clarify how those boundaries reflect God's purposes and not simply our personal preferences.

18. Richard Lischer, *Open Secrets* (New York: Random House, 2001), p. 204.

Resurrecting Friendships for Pastoral Leaders

When we began asking groups of pastors and laity what was most important in sustaining their work, friendship was almost always at the top of the list. A clear sense of purpose, supportive family, able judicatory leadership, and adequate financial resources for a life well lived are all important. But the need for good friends seems to transcend the challenges and frustrations that plague so many. Conversations about and among friends persistently awaken and enliven even the dullest gathering.

One explanation, of course, is that friendships bring to mind a face, a particular conversation, a unique story. Pastors talk about the friends who first encouraged them to consider ordained ministry as a vocation, and friends to whom they have turned and continue to turn for the advice, perspective, accountability, and encouragement that sustain that vocation. Conversations about salary schedules, pension funds, clergy deployment, and mission strategies can sometimes be so general as to be obscure, but recollections of friendship are usually particular, even poignant.

Yet numerous studies over the past two decades have documented a longstanding problem with clergy loneliness. As recently as 2001, the Pulpit & Pew national survey discovered that only about one-third of the clergy interviewed said they had never felt lonely or isolated. Indeed, "loneliness and isolation" was the single greatest predictor of overall job dissatisfaction among Protestants and Catholics, according to that 2001 survey.

In both implicit and explicit descriptions of the clergy's vocation in contemporary America, we are guided *not* to think about friendship — especially with laity. Bring up the topic of holy friendships among a group of pastors, and the conversation will quickly turn to clergy-parishioner friendships. "Can't be done." That's the consensus of most clergy. These pastors argue that friendships within the parish will lead to resentment, misunderstanding, and, ultimately, heartache. For the sake of the office, the congregation, and one's family, they argue, clergy should not become friends with church members.

Many laity — often including the pastor's spouse and children — find this argument surprising and very odd. If holy friendships are central to a community's life, why should the pastor be exempt? After all, the pastor often participates in the most intimate moments of celebration and sorrow in a person's life — birth, baptism, wedding, divorce, and death. If a person who shares in all of this is not a friend, who is? Moreover, when so much time is devoted to a particular community, how does one *not* become a friend? The Gospels are filled with stories describing Jesus' friendship with his followers. As one pastor asked, "Who are we ministers to declare that our roles are somehow more complicated?"

It is true that a therapeutic model of ministry has cautioned against these friendships, defining the pastor's role as similar to that of the analyst or counselor. Better to find friendships apart from the people who are being served. And, to be fair, spiritual leaders such as Teresa of Ávila also warned of the consequences that special friendships can pose within one's religious community. But much of the controversy about these friendships seems to be more closely linked to the definitions of friendship.

"A friend is someone with whom I can share everything," one pastor argued, "and there is no way I can share everything with a parishioner. I know things about people in my church that others in the congregation shouldn't know — about money, about marital infidelity, about problems with children. I don't want a member thinking I'm going to run off and tell my friend who also is a member." We agree. But we'd also challenge that premise of friendship. Are friends, especially holy friends, people with whom we share *everything?*

It is helpful to reframe the discussion, as Lillian Daniel did for our colloquium, in terms of Christian practice: "If holy friendship is a practice of the faith, then it will be shaped and limited by a community over time. In practices, not anything goes. Guidelines keep us within the boundaries of our tradition and our faith."[19] There are times when holy friendship requires speaking difficult truths plainly. It does not mean that we articulate every thought, especially if those thoughts do not serve the holy alliances of the community.

In the church we hope to be able to share stories of our children's addictions, our spouse's job loss, even our painful betrayals without intimidation, accusation, or further harm. We also hope to be able to share stories of great joys and good news. But we do not need to share

---

19. Daniel, "Rough Edges of Holy Friendship," p. 7.

everything. Our friendships are learned and lived as a practice of our life in Christ, an awareness that also acknowledges that we do not share everything. As Daniel noted: "By considering holy friendship to be a practice of faith, we acknowledge what our culture denies but what most of us know to be true: limits can strengthen friendship with one another and with God."[20]

We suggest that questions about holy friendships among clergy and laity have less to do with *whether* we participate in these relationships and more to do with *how* we live in the midst of such friendships. How do we honor the intimacies and information we share with one another? How do we acknowledge that in the community of faith, our friendships choose us as much as we choose them? How do clergy and laity hold one another accountable in these relationships and learn to welcome and let go of one another as transitions take place?

Holy friendships among clergy and laity are complex, but no more so than other relationships involving a mutual effort to be faithful to the communities God has given us. Daniel reminded us that clergy and laity would do well to recall the strained relationship between Moses and his people as they tried to maintain a holy friendship in the desert:

> So Moses said to the LORD, "Why have you treated your servant so badly? Why have I not found favor in your sight that you lay the burden of all this people on me? . . . I am not able to carry all this people alone, for they are too heavy for me." (Num. 11:11, 14)

Daniel urged pastors who think they are in charge to listen closely to the story. "God compels Moses to reach out to the 70 elders with whom he has clearly lost touch. God reminds Moses that he must be in relationship with them, not simply for his own benefit. . . . This friendship will lead to God's work being done."[21]

It is also crucial that pastors cultivate holy friendships with other pastors, their peers. Often this works better outside the confines of one denomination, as too often "priestly fellowship" can degenerate into gripe sessions. But an authentic set of peer friendships can be a critically important source of sustenance for faithful Christian living.

20. Daniel, "Rough Edges of Holy Friendship," p. 8.
21. Daniel, "Rough Edges of Holy Friendship," p. 9.

Many clergy are discovering the significance of peer groups in order to overcome the loneliness and isolation that is diminishing their effectiveness and, too often, damaging their sense of hope and vitality. Yet these groups need the depth of commitment found in holy friendships, and they also need a sense of eschatological direction — they need to be centered in God and focused on God's kingdom.

In our colloquium Kyle Childress described his group of clergy friends, affectionately known as "the neighborhood." For the last dozen years, six Texas pastors have been gathering twice a year for several days away from their families, their churches, their cell phones, and their computers. They gather simply to be with one another. Over time, they have learned to talk about vocational struggles, parenting difficulties and marital stress, frustration and loneliness and exhaustion, and problems of rivalry and selfish ambition — including with each other. They have challenged one another's sins they had come to love, affirmed gifts they were afraid to claim, and helped one another dream dreams they otherwise would not have dreamed.

Childress also notes the deeper appreciation of ministry these friendships have produced, and of the diverse ways in which faithful Christian leadership is exercised. "Our deeper conversations," he writes, "remind us that we are different kinds of pastors with different perspectives and approaches to our common vocation. Charlie preaches to 2,000 people every Sunday morning while I preach to 90. He has a strong CEO streak, while I approach the call like a farmer. We have a lot to learn from one another. I am learning that not all big-steeple pastors are ambitious religious capitalists; he is learning that small congregation pastors are not necessarily lazy underachievers. He's no Enron executive; I'm no Snuffy Smith."[22]

* * *

Living "alongside" requires an eschatological community and imagination. The contours and complexities of our relationships are never fully revealed to us all at once. We do not know ourselves well

---

22. Kyle Childress, "Company of Friends: Six Pastors Make a Sabbath," SPE Web site, http://www.divinity.duke.edu/programs/spe/resources/tcc-companyfriends.html. This article also appeared in *The Christian Century* (April 6, 2004).

enough, nor are we usually confident enough, to disclose ourselves instantly to others in a truth-full manner. Moreover, we will likely be skeptical of and resistant to those who insist on trying to do so. Relationships rhythmically unfold and develop like the seasons.

There are times when we demand more of our friendships and more is demanded of us. There are other times when our friendships appear fallow. Holy friendships require a bifocal vision: an ability to attend to what is at hand while also looking to what lies ahead.

So many of our relationships are malnourished because they survive on fast food and transient encounters. We have little time to know each other *as friends,* rather than as committee members, sports competitors, social activists, or carpool captains. We squeeze in conversations on the sidelines of the soccer field, or in the express lane of the supermarket. By contrast, honest self-disclosure and truthful encounters require an active waiting and undistracted presence that allows our friendships to take root, strangers to be welcomed, and enemies to be named and loved.

"No longer do I call you servants," Jesus says to his disciples in the farewell passages of John's Gospel. "I call you friends, because I have made known to you everything that I have heard from my Father." Holy friendships have a larger purpose beyond the relationship itself: holy friendships point us toward God. They allow us to discover and reveal the abundant grace of God at work in our lives and in the world.

The vocation of Christian life is learned, lived, and sustained through holy friendships and faithful practices that open us to God's grace. Yet within the vocation of Christian life there is a particular vocation, the vocation of pastoral leadership, which is indispensable for helping to shape and sustain the vocation of all Christians. We turn to exploration of that vocation in the next chapter.

4 Resurrecting Excellence in the Pastoral Vocation

In order to fulfil its mission, the Church needs persons who are publicly and continually responsible for pointing to its fundamental dependence on Jesus Christ, and thereby provide, within a multiplicity of gifts, a focus of its unity. The ministry of such persons, who since very early times have been ordained, is constitutive for the life and witness of the Church.[1]

Since the earliest days of the church, persons have been set aside by the community and called by God — and, typically, ordained — "to build up the community in Christ and to strengthen its witness."[2] Through such activities as proclaiming the gospel, celebrating the sacraments, leading and ordering the community, equipping the saints for ministry, and engaging the world in outreach and witness, these persons enable the ministry of all Christians. Called to be exemplars

1. *Baptism, Eucharist, and Ministry,* Faith and Order Paper 111 (Geneva: World Council of Churches, 1982), paragraph M8. Christians among the divided churches have different ways of understanding the specific shape of ordering ministry and the role of the ordained. We are relying here on the ecumenical document *Baptism, Eucharist, and Ministry (BEM),* which has received widespread acclaim from diverse Christian communities, to articulate the heart of the calling to ordained ministry. We acknowledge that not all Christians will agree with our descriptions; however, we have sought to describe the need for ordained pastoral leadership in terms that will be as broadly shared as possible.

2. *Baptism, Eucharist, and Ministry,* paragraph M12.

of holiness and loving concern, they are asked to become more than they already are. Indeed, those who are called to the vocation of pastoral leadership are asked to represent on behalf of the community that to which all the people of God are called.

"Those who carry the vessels of the Lord," Gregory the Great once wrote, "are those who undertake, in reliance on their way of living, to draw the souls of their neighbors to the everlasting holy places."[3] Those who become clergy are called to be preachers and teachers, sacramental presiders, and leaders who reflect the light of Christ in a way that becomes compelling, even beautiful, to their neighbors. Theirs is a vocation to a life of creativity and growth in holy living, a life that emerges from the intersections of our lives, the life of the world, and God's life. Those entrusted with ordained ministry are called to a life that is deeply attractive, even in its risks, because it takes with utmost seriousness the mystery and complexity of both human and divine life. It is a way of living that, through example, careful study, and gifts of leadership, is able to draw others to the light of God's kingdom, to the "everlasting holy places" — places of mercy, compassion, and justice; places of beauty, joy, and salvation. It is a deeply human way of living that is "filled with all the fullness of God" (Eph. 3:19).

A Three-Dimensional Vision

At different times in the history of Christianity, and even today among diverse and divided communities of Christians, there have been very different understandings of the vocation of ordained pastoral leadership. Three basic theological understandings of ordained ministry — as calling, profession, and office — are often taken to be in conflict. Put in vastly oversimplified terms, there are two "default" sensibilities that often implicitly underlie the discussions about the shape and ordering of pastoral ministry: in one view, a "high church" sensibility, the pastor is sent from God to serve as the mediator of God's word in the pulpit and the sacramental presider in Christ's stead at the table; in the other view, a "low church" sensibility, the pastor is called out

3. Gregory the Great, *Pastoral Care*, trans. Henry Davis, S.J. (New York: Newman, 1950), 2.2, p. 46.

from the community to serve particular functions that the community needs to have fulfilled.[4]

Will Willimon rightly notes that we need not choose between the two. In his words, "Both views have scriptural basis and historical precedent. The first stresses the gifted, grace-filled quality of ministry as a special gift of God to the church. The second asserts the functional, community-derived quality of Christian ministry."[5]

Even so, as understandings of ordained pastoral leadership have developed over the centuries, and now in the midst of divided communities of Christians, these default sensibilities have emerged in disagreements about a whole range of issues: whether there ought to be bishops, whether women ought be ordained, what the educational and instructional requirements for ministers should be, whether ordination is primarily about the stamping of a particular character on the person or an affirmation of particular functions to be fulfilled, and, related to these, whether the requisite "gifts" needed to serve as an ordained pastoral leader should be focused on continuity with traditional understandings, the depth of one's relationship with God, intellectual and practical competence, particular traits of character, or the capacity to perform particular functions well.

Obviously, any tradition hopes that people do not have to choose among these gifts, that pastoral leaders will have a constellation of gifts that includes them all. Yet our understandings of pastoral leadership do inform debates about particular issues and specific cases that present themselves, often in confused and confusing ways because we are unaware of them. We believe that confusion about the vocation of pastoral leadership can lead to distorted understandings that, over time, conspire to weaken the church, the discipleship of all Christians, and the ministry of those called to lead. At the same time, we believe that clarity about the theological understandings of ordination can illumine all Christian ministry and help resurrect excellence in the pastoral vocation.

4. David Bartlett characterizes these as the two major options that people today describe, and suggests that both of them have merit in relation to the New Testament. See his book *Ministry in the New Testament* (Minneapolis: Fortress, 1993). See also the discussion in William H. Willimon, *Pastor: The Theology and Practice of Ordained Ministry* (Nashville: Abingdon, 2002), pp. 38-39.

5. Willimon, *Pastor*, p. 39.

Later in this chapter we will take up the matter of distortions, followed by a more fulsome description of the wholeness of pastoral ministry as discovered through the intersecting capacities and gifts of calling, profession, and office. But first we turn to a brief outline of these three understandings, suggesting that each has something important to contribute to the shaping of faithful Christian ministry.[6]

Calling

The understanding of ordained ministry as a calling is particularly concerned with the spiritual depth and maturity of pastoral leaders. The focus is on the irreplaceable significance of the call from God, the spiritual fire and depth that come from encounter and ongoing relationship with God. Certainly a sense of calling has been important to the other models of ministry, especially a sense of being called to a particular office. Those who understand the pastoral vocation as primarily a calling, however, would argue that a person can occupy an office or be educated in a profession yet lack the essential Christian passion and commitment that can only come from a clear, distinctive call. So Gilbert Tennent, for example, preaching in the eighteenth century, compared an "unconverted" minister with "a man who would learn others to swim before he'd learned it himself, and so is drowned in the Act and dies like a fool. . . ."[7]

We can illumine this concern for ordained ministry as a calling by turning to H. Richard Niebuhr's classic description of "the call to ministry" in his book *The Purpose of the Church and Its Ministry*. Niebuhr identifies four basic elements in the call:

1. *The call to be a Christian,* that is, "the call to discipleship of Jesus Christ, to hearing and doing the Word of God, to repentance and faith"
2. *The secret call,* "that inner persuasion or experience whereby a

---

6. See also Jackson W. Carroll, *God's Potters* (Grand Rapids: Eerdmans, 2006), chapter 1, for a more extended discussion of calling, profession, and office as they bear on contemporary models of ministry. We draw on Carroll's analysis in our own descriptions, even as we emphasize theological rather than sociological concerns.

7. Cited in Carroll, *God's Potters*, typescript p. I-30.

person feels himself [or herself] directly summoned or invited by God to take up the work of the ministry"

3. *The providential call,* "that invitation and command to assume the work of the ministry which comes through the equipment of a person with the talents necessary for the exercise of the office and through the divine guidance of his life by all its circumstances"

4. *The ecclesiastical call,* "the summons and invitation extended to a man [or woman] by some community or institution of the Church to engage in the work of the ministry"[8]

Niebuhr's description fits the model of ordained ministry as a calling. It arises out of the call of all Christians to follow Jesus through discipleship, and it is particularly focused on a person's distinctive sense that she has been *directly* summoned by God.

Ideally, all four elements converge in a person's call to serve as an ordained pastor. But what happens if there is a gap, or a conflict among them? In many circumstances through the history of Christianity, people who have experienced a calling to ordained leadership, often expressed as a call to preach, have lacked the confirmation of what Niebuhr terms "the ecclesiastical call" — often because of gender, race, or ethnicity.

Some who see ordained ministry as primarily a calling have held that the call is all that is needed. This view has emerged particularly in some Pentecostal and other traditions that emphasize evangelism and being attuned to new life in the Spirit, and more recently in what have been identified as "new paradigm" churches. In this conception, God does not call the equipped but rather equips the called.

Critics of ordained ministry understood only as a calling have stressed that unless there are external standards by which a calling is tested and confirmed, we lack the means to discern whether a person is truly called by God through the power of the Holy Spirit. A person may be called by other spirits, demonic and otherwise. Other critics have stressed that a profound sense of personal calling is necessary but not sufficient to sustain pastoral leadership over time. Those who

8. H. Richard Niebuhr, *The Purpose of the Church and Its Ministry* (New York: Harper, 1956), p. 64.

are truly called to become pastoral leaders must cultivate a sense of the office and of the education and competence needed to flourish in service to the Christian community.

Even so, ordained ministry understood as a calling provides a critically important source of renewal for the church. A sense of calling is indispensable to discerning Christian vocation; it provides an awareness of the Spirit's work in challenging tendencies toward institutional rigidity and accommodation to worldly standards that are marked by sin; and it enables fresh understandings of the particular gifts with which God equips those whom God calls to pastoral leadership. After all, those who are entrusted with leadership by God in Scripture are often those who would otherwise seem to lack standing.

Profession

The understanding of pastoral ministry as a profession is rooted in the importance of education and training for the practice of a vocation. The education involved is designed to provide specialized knowledge and understanding, whereas the training emphasizes mastery of the skills needed to practice the vocation well. Such a model is especially apt for those Christian traditions, such as classical Protestantism, that stress the centrality of preaching and teaching and thus desire a learned clergy. On this understanding, the clergy are expected to be competent professionals capable of leading wisely and of providing particular services to the community.

The emphasis on ordained ministry as a profession has become increasingly prevalent in the United States since the beginning of the nineteenth century. Prior to that time, the notion of "professionals" — primarily doctors, lawyers, and clergy — had more to do with social status in a hierarchically ordered society than with a distinctive shaping for a vocation.[9] Through the nineteenth and twentieth centuries, the vocations of doctors, lawyers, and clergy became associated with the need for specialized knowledge, training, and service for their constituencies as they addressed fundamental human problems.

9. We are grateful to Jackson Carroll and Brooks Holifield for helping us see and articulate these points.

Even prior to the nineteenth century, there was a keen sense of the importance of education for the profession of ministry. Many of the leading universities in the United States, including Harvard, began as institutions for educating clergy. During the last two hundred years, this emphasis on ministry as a profession has resulted in the creation and expansion of seminary education as essential for ordained ministry. There have been tensions between those traditions that have emphasized a more classical understanding of education and those that have stressed a schooling in particular functions and skills. But the traditions have typically shared, at least until recently, a commitment to formal education and training as important for the clergy's vocation.

There are valuable themes and insights associated with an emphasis on ordained ministry as a profession. After all, the very notion of a "profession" has roots in religious orders, and in its original conception signified a person who had committed his or her whole life to service. Moreover, even contemporary accounts of professions have tended to emphasize standards of excellence, advanced study, service to a community, and codes of ethics.

Even so, the "professional" model of ordained ministry has had a persistent and growing chorus of critics. Some of the criticism has been directed at a "culture of professionalism" more generally, suggesting that it has distanced the professions from their communities in service of a class-based elitism that functions more to perpetuate its own sense of specialized knowledge and training than anything else.[10] But the criticism has also been directed at the fact that a "profession of ministry" can easily be described and maintained apart from any convictions about God, any commitment to a distinctive community patterned in the life, death, and resurrection of Jesus, any awareness of the responsibility to serve the laity in their vocations, or any directedness toward the coming kingdom of God.

Still, even critics of the professional model affirm the importance of education, standards of excellence in knowledge and skill, and the significance of service to a community.

10. For an excellent overview of the issues, see Burton J. Bledstein's important book *The Culture of Professionalism* (New York: Norton, 1976).

Office

Theologically, the understanding of the pastoral vocation as an office has been a way of emphasizing that the clergy represent Christ in and for the community — in preaching the word, celebrating the sacraments, and ordering the life of the church — as well as in and for the world. Central to this understanding is the clergyperson's character, or holiness. We see this, for example, in Gregory the Great's specification of the clergy's "reliance on their way of living" as being critical to "draw[ing] the souls of their neighbors to the everlasting holy places."

An emphasis on the representational role, properly understood, avoids the false alternatives that the clerical office *depends* upon the character of the person in the office or (a claim often made after discovering egregious failings in a particular clergyperson) that such character is irrelevant. Rather, the representational role, understood as an office, is located in bearing witness to Christ and the coming fullness of God's inbreaking kingdom. Such an emphasis stresses the purpose of the church and its ministry as service to the Triune God through lives centered in Christ, and the direction and *telos* of that service in relation to God's reign.

To be sure, all Christians are to imitate Christ, but those set aside as ordained clergy are to live exemplary lives that serve to model, inspire, and encourage imitation and emulation by others. So, for example, in services of ordination, people becoming pastors are often asked, "Will you adorn the doctrine of Our Savior by a holy life and conversation?"[11] By answering in the affirmative, the clergy promise to live lives in the pursuit of holiness, to be exemplary leaders for the calling of the whole church, and all disciples, to holiness.

The clergy are thus called to commit themselves to growing into the office that they occupy — in other words, to diminishing the gaps between their character and the definitive exemplar, Jesus Christ. Richard John Neuhaus's assessment is instructive: "The office that is entrusted to us inescapably carries with it that obligation and privi-

---

11. This particular formulation is drawn from the Lutheran tradition. See the discussion in Richard John Neuhaus, *Freedom for Ministry* (New York: Harper & Row, 1979), pp. 185ff.

lege of exemplification. The ongoing task is to strengthen the coherence between 'office' and 'person'; in other words, the person is to 'adorn' the office."[12]

While the theological emphasis of "office" has been on the importance of the clergy's character, or holiness, it is important to acknowledge that, to the extent that the "officialness" of the office is stressed, the particularity of the clergyperson has tended to diminish. Hence, one worry with an exclusive or primary understanding of ordained ministry as an office is that, ironically, the individual character or effectiveness of the clergy can actually be deemphasized. For example, there has been a persistent criticism through the history of the church, especially vocal in the Middle Ages, that the clergy lack appropriate character and education. For these critics, the clergy occupy an office as "representatives," but their character is not exemplary, nor are they gifted at carrying out the functions of pastoral leadership.

In modernity, partly in response to the ineffectiveness of many clergy, and especially among those with more "low church" sensibilities, the understanding of the pastoral vocation as an "office" has been associated more with specific functions that need to be performed and less with the "representative" character of the person who performs them. But even in those traditions in which a functional model tends to predominate, as well as those in which the emphasis is not placed on "office" at all, there still tends to be at least a residual sense that those set aside to serve as clergy ought to be exemplars of holy living in order to encourage the larger community.

*   *   *

We are convinced that the church is more likely to bear witness to a resurrecting excellence in Christian ministry if we stress the overlapping strengths and mutually reinforcing complementarity of the three models of the pastoral vocation. Diverse traditions and theological sensibilities about ordination will undoubtedly lead to an emphasis on one of these understandings over the others — so, for example, free church and evangelical traditions are more likely to emphasize the significance of calling; mainline traditions, profession; and liturgi-

12. Neuhaus, *Freedom for Ministry,* p. 188.

cal and "high-church" traditions, office. But the richest and most coherent conceptions and practices of pastoral leadership will emphasize one while drawing on the strengths of the other two. When the
three understandings work together well, they cultivate the kind of
resurrecting excellence in the pastoral vocation that Christian communities need — leaders who, in reliance on their way of feeling,
thinking, and acting, draw the souls of their neighbors to the "everlasting holy places."

Distortions of the Pastoral Vocation

The vocation of pastoral leadership flourishes when it draws on the
mutually reinforcing understandings of calling, profession, and office.
All three perspectives are needed if we are to be faithful to the witness
of Scripture and the insights of our forebears, to the wisdom of what
both inaugurates and sustains institutions, and to the life of discipleship in God's inbreaking kingdom. Indeed, over time it is difficult to
maintain a coherent sense of the purpose and *telos* of the church — a
purpose that arises out of the church's vocation to equip the saints for
ministry and make disciples of all people, and a *telos* that is the kingdom of God — apart from the interrelations of calling, profession, and
office in the vocation of pastoral leadership.

When we lose a sense of the purpose and *telos* of ordained ministry, we find ourselves in degenerating spirals of distorted identities,
practices, and systems. As those spirals move downward, they begin
to obscure the character and gifts of the persons we most need to be
setting aside for ordained leadership; moreover, these distortions begin to fester in ways that diminish and undermine even those faithful
and effective clergy we have set aside who could otherwise be flourishing.

Distorted identities, practices, and systems are related, respec-
tively, to the models of calling, profession, and office. At their worst,
they produce mirror opposites of their vibrant theological counter-
parts. Thus calling degenerates into therapy; profession into
careerism; and office into hierarchy and bureaucracy. The loss of
Christian purpose and direction in one contributes to loss in the other
two, and over time they reinforce a nontheological, disconnected set

of understandings of the pastoral vocation that is evidenced in ministries of mediocrity — or of outright destruction.

Calling and Its Distortion into Therapy

One of the most basic capacities for persons discerning a vocation to Christian leadership is a keen sense of their own identities, their strengths and limitations, their potential for sin as well as for holy living. The clergy, no less than the laity, face the challenge of discerning "who they are" over time. They are not exempt from the dangers of sinful distortions of their own identities or their relations to others. Indeed, given the power that is entrusted to the clergy, a capacity for critical and constructive self-awareness is absolutely crucial.

Such a critical and constructive self-awareness is one of the gifts that comes from spiritual disciplines, a life in which one learns to listen carefully to God through prayer and through holy friendships with others. Yet too often people turn to particular jobs, including ordained ministry, more as a way of avoiding coming to terms with themselves than anything else.

People in positions of power need to have enough of a sense of "who they are" that they do not act out of their own needs and hurts. Obvious failures in this regard have been manifest in egregious examples of sexual or financial misconduct on the part of clergy. Yet the failures are no less damaging to congregations when they are more subtle, manifested in excessive bids for control, attention, or validation.

Unfortunately, in recent decades we have allowed the rich Christian tradition of "calling" for laity and clergy to degenerate into self-initiated searches for work. While for many people that becomes an external preoccupation with career, money, and prestige, for others it becomes an internal preoccupation with their own woundedness.

Ironically, Henri Nouwen's theologically rich conception of clergy as "wounded healers" has contributed to the problem.[13] Nouwen's own argument has significant and rich implications. He structures it to note the interrelations of the conditions of a suffering world, a suffering generation, a suffering person, and a suffering minister.

13. Henri J. M. Nouwen, *The Wounded Healer* (Garden City, N.Y.: Doubleday, 1972).

Nouwen offers insights into the ways woundedness can shape a faithful ministry patterned in the life, death, and resurrection of Jesus Christ.

Nouwen's basic point has broad relevance. After all, God often works most powerfully in our lives at the location of our wounds, whether they are the result of our own doing, of tragedy, or of the sinful behavior of others. So, for example, the Reverend Bill Ritter has taken the tragedy of his son's suicide as an opportunity to minister in profoundly beautiful ways to families who have likewise suffered a loved one's suicide. In numerous conversations and pastoral settings, in a series of five sermons preached to his congregation during the decade after his son's death, and subsequently in the gift of a book that offers those sermons more widely, Ritter has embodied the kind of "wounded healer" who has helped others place their wounds into the wounds of the crucified and resurrected Christ.[14]

In a very different context, social activist John Perkins discovered a powerful sense of his vocation as a Christian and a minister by locating his woundedness from years of abuse in the wounds of Christ. An African American born in 1930 in Mississippi, Perkins suffered growing up in a Jim Crow society. In his adulthood, his wounds became physical as well as spiritual and emotional, as he endured harassment, beatings, and imprisonment at the hands of the Klan and other white racists — including a beating in jail that almost cost him his life. Despite his vocation as a minister, and despite his social activism, Perkins found himself developing an overwhelming sense of hatred for whites and anger at how he had been treated.

In 1970, after more than ten years of ministry in Mississippi, Perkins became ill with heart disease, ulcers, and other ailments related to his beatings. Moreover, he had reached a state of deep personal despair. He felt that whites deserved his hatred, and he struggled with Jesus' teaching to "do good to them that hate you." As he grappled with his illness and his despair, he finally allowed the full hatred in his soul to come to the surface. Charles Marsh describes the result as follows: "As [Perkins] did an image took shape in his mind. 'The image of the cross,' he said, 'Christ on the cross. It blotted out

---

14. See William A. Ritter, *Take the Dimness of My Soul Away* (Harrisburg, Pa.: Morehouse, 2004).

everything else in my mind.' Jesus was a Savior who had been tortured and murdered by a lynch mob, 'nailed to rough wooden planks,' and 'killed like a common criminal.' Jesus had been born homeless in poverty and deserted by his father at the moment of his greatest need. The image of Christ's suffering for the world worked its way into the center of his thoughts, fears, and humiliations, and Perkins came to a new understanding of his life's work."[15]

By locating his wounds in the wounds of Christ, Perkins discovered a purpose and direction for his life. Since that time, Perkins has been a major leader in racial reconciliation and Christian community development through his Voice of Calvary Ministries in Mississippi and other efforts across the country. His story exemplifies the power of a theologically rich "wounded healer."

Unfortunately, Nouwen's image of the "wounded healer" has too often been disconnected from the pattern of Christ's dying and rising. And that has allowed people to center themselves in their own wounds — and then return regularly to lick them. The notion of a wounded healer has too often degenerated into a pop-psychology definition of woundedness as a crucial criterion for ordained ministry. As a result, we have allowed and even encouraged needy people who don't know "who they are" to become entrusted with leadership of congregations. The repercussions have been problematic at best, and terribly destructive at worst.

A thirteen-year-old boy identified this problem in relation to his own pastor with penetrating insight. After church one day, he remarked to his mother: "You know, mom, the trouble with our new pastor is that he needs us to love him so much that we can't see God anymore." The new pastor had arrived and, in a rather short time, had torn apart the fabric of Christian community that had been nurtured in that congregation over several decades.

Most of the adults had identified the problem as something else: an authoritarian leadership style, too many changes in worship practices, an inability to listen, an unwillingness to understand the congregation's distinctive history. But once this young teenager described

15. Charles Marsh, *The Beloved Community* (New York: Basic Books, 2005), pp. 171-72. Marsh devotes a chapter of this important book to Perkins's story. We are grateful to Craig Kocher for drawing our attention to this particular passage and its significance.

the issue in terms of the pastor's neediness, the other descriptions fell into place.

"We can't see God anymore." Well, not technically — after all, whether at the table or in the pulpit, the presence of God does not depend on the holiness of the priest or pastor. This has been the judgment of the church since the resolution of the Donatist controversy at the beginning of the fifth century. But this young teenager wasn't expressing a technical theological point. He was simply suggesting that it is much more difficult to worship God when ordained ministers are so preoccupied with themselves and their own needs that God is relegated to the sidelines.

Self-absorbed ministry issues from a pastor's lack of Christian character. Whether a matter of an excessive estimation of one's own importance or a sense of weakness and insecurity, everything revolves around the pastor's need to be the focus of attention and affirmation. This focus becomes even more pernicious if it is couched in terms that sound like Christian faithfulness. So a pastor preaches a sermon on "Humility and How I Achieved It" or sings as if the "Blessed Assurance" is not so much "praising my Savior all the day long" as "this is MY story." A *Kudzu* cartoon has the Reverend Will B. Dunn answering a multiple-choice question: "What is the Holy Trinity? (A) Father, Son, and Holy Ghost; (B) Me, Myself, and I." In the final frame, Rev. Dunn muses, "This must be a trick question."[16]

It becomes difficult to see God when needy pastors focus the attention on themselves and their own wounds. While it is true that all Christians bear wounds, and that those wounds can give rise to powerful ministry, it is also the case that our calling is to place our wounds into the wounds of Christ. It is particularly important for pastoral leaders to do so, as was powerfully emphasized by a church official in Rwanda during a visit there. Reflecting on the fact that most pastoral leaders in Rwanda were directly affected by the genocide there, he noted that "in Rwanda we have wounded leaders." But, he added, "leaders must be healed of those wounds in order to lead others in the healing of their wounds." He paused, and then said, "Unfortunately, leaders are often the last ones to acknowledge their wounds, because it takes humility and vulnerability to do so." That is why all

16. Doug Marlette, *Kudzu*, July 6, 2005.

Christians, and especially pastoral leaders, are called to bear witness to Christ's dying and rising: the focus is on the power of Christ, not on ourselves. As Paul writes in the Letter to the Galatians, "I have been crucified with Christ; and it is no longer I who live, but it is Christ who lives in me" (Gal. 2:19-20).

In addition to the misguided notions of pop psychology, certain contemporary structures and expectations of pastoral leaders have reinforced the appeal of a therapeutic conception of calling. We have allowed a "lone ranger" mentality to emerge among clergy for a variety of competitive, legal, and bureaucratic reasons. But a lone ranger lacks the ecologies of support, holy friendships, and community that sustain a faithful and ever-deepening understanding of one's calling. Such a mentality leads to a preoccupation with oneself in destructive ways.

Furthermore, the character of ordained ministry as a life-giving calling is undermined when it is experienced as a never-ending, low-paying job. Impossible expectations placed on clergy by denominations, congregations, and cultural stereotypes lead some to think that ordained ministry is about denying oneself the satisfactions and rewards of other vocations. This attracts those whose needs are less vocational or material and more characterological. Hence, emotionally needy people are especially drawn to the status and practice of contemporary ordained ministry.

We have confused the recognition that Christian life is for *all persons* about dying to self and rising with Christ with the misguided (yet often subtly hidden) assumption that ordained ministers are the designated "self-deniers." As a result, the conditions are ripe for difficulty in a sense of calling even among Christian leaders of good character and self-awareness.

Why are we surprised when even healthy and faithful pastors become excessively needy if they are lonely and isolated, or struggling with concerns about how to care for their children's education or their own retirement? Or if they feel that their work is not honored? Why do we so often ignore the importance of friendships, material resources, and educational and cultural opportunities as ingredients in a life well lived for pastors and their families? It is no wonder that a discouraged pastor started delivering a lecture entitled "Mamas, Don't Let Your Babies Grow Up to Be Preachers."

Profession and Its Distortion into Careerism

These contemporary structures and expectations contribute as well to the degeneration of profession into professionalized career, and of office into hierarchy and bureaucracy. Seen from a "professionalized" perspective, it becomes discouraging to realize how little clergy are paid for our work, particularly in relation to doctors, lawyers, business people, and even other lower-paid professionals such as teachers and social workers.[17] And, disconnected from a sense of purpose and direction, our work as "uncredentialed" politicians, businesspersons, therapists, sociologists, and teachers seems discouragingly ineffective, unrewarding, and indeed insignificant. There is no question that the profession of contemporary ministry is, in many ways, in crisis. But Richard Lischer challenged our colloquium to consider the true nature of the crisis:

> Usually, when Christians speak of a crisis in ministry, they mean a professional crisis, one that can be measured by declining competencies, falling morale, sliding salaries, and other indices of grief. These are solvable problems.
>
> A vocational crisis, on the other hand, is neither solvable nor a problem. . . . We cannot undo the new and sometimes bewildering historical and technological contexts of ministry, nor even rectify our own alienation from its traditional duties. Thank God it *is* a vocational crisis we are dealing with because the word "vocation," call, makes space for *God* in our self-assessment. In fact, it makes no sense to speak of vocation *unless* one believes in a God who is still capable of summoning people into partnership.[18]

As partners with God, surely we should be empowered to excel in the rigors and standards of our holy profession. And we are empowered to excel — but it is toward *resurrecting* excellence. Lischer continued:

---

17. See Becky R. McMillan and Matthew J. Price, *How Much Should We Pay the Pastor? A Fresh Look at Clergy Salaries,* Pulpit & Pew Research Reports (Winter 2003).

18. Richard Lischer, "The Ministry of the Word" (Colloquium on Excellence in Ministry, Duke Divinity School, Durham, N.C., September 19-20, 2002), p. 2; see also Lischer, *The End of Words: The Language of Reconciliation in a Culture of Violence* (Grand Rapids: Eerdmans, 2005).

What distinguishes a vocation from the rigors and standards of a profession is this: you have to die to enter a vocation. A profession brings out the best in you. A vocation calls you away from what you *thought* was best in you, purifies it, and promises to make you something or someone you are not yet.

In the Bible, God's call invades the most sacrosanct spaces of the human person. You get a new name. Racial and sexual labels give way to a new identity. Physical or linguistic disabilities that defined you from birth are refigured. Family relationships may be severed, occupations forsaken. A vocation puts an end to you in order to disclose your true end.[19]

J. F. Powers satirizes a professionalized conception of ordained ministry in his novel *Wheat That Springeth Green*.[20] Joe Hackett is a Roman Catholic priest who has given up his desire for holiness (he confused sanctity with sanctimony in the seminary), and has accommodated himself to a professionalized, worldly understanding of his work as pastor of a suburban parish. Joe is a "builder" of programs who is "managing" the parish, and he is quite proud of the fiscal system he has installed. He indicates that "we don't talk about [money] here — in church. We just present the bill for services rendered, like doctors and lawyers." He reflects that his congregants are too busy worrying about public relations to even *want* to be saints.[21] No longer concerned with holy living or leading a congregation in bearing witness to God's kingdom, Joe has become a moderately successful professional.

Those activities that used to be a regular part of Joe's life have become foreign to him. Prayer and meditation no longer interest him much; he fears that both God and he would be bored. Even the public activities of the ministerial office that he is expected to fulfill have become oddly disconnected from his self-understanding and no longer seem very important — activities such as celebrating the sacraments, preaching, offering spiritual direction, ministering among the poor, leading his congregation in their discipleship.

Even in the midst of his professionalized ministry, however, Joe

19. Lischer, "Ministry of the Word," p. 3; see Lischer, *End of Words*, p. 30.
20. J. F. Powers, *Wheat That Springeth Green* (New York: Knopf, 1988).
21. Powers, *Wheat That Springeth Green*, pp. 151, 198.

carries with him a lingering sense that his vocation as a pastor ought to be different. He senses that the clergy ought to be persons of character who reflect Christ's holiness, provide wise counsel, and nurture people in the waters of salvation. But he notes that they are unable to do so because, like beached whales, they are mired in mud. The mud is partly of their own making, and partly a product of distorted conceptions and expectations from the church in general and laity in particular.

Joe tells some of his fellow priests that he is aware of frequent reports, like those of flying saucers, of parishes where the clergy and people are doing great things together. "But I've never seen one myself, if it's any consolation to you guys."[22] Focused on their professionalized careers, they have lost the eyes to see and ears to hear the beauty and excellence of Christian life — of congregations and clergy doing great things together, bearing witness to the Holy Spirit's work in the world.

Mired in mud, Joe and his fellow priests feel thwarted, useless, and demoralized. He has a recurring problem with alcohol and a profound sense of loneliness and isolation. He even questions his vocation. Yet he yearns for a renewed sense of calling, an appreciation of the vocation to the priesthood. Over time, he begins to turn again to themes such as the imitation of Christ and the centrality of the cross.

While on a vacation in Canada, Joe's life takes a new turn. He describes himself to a priest as an "office manager" in a "branch office" of a "multinational concern."[23] The priest asks him to think about whether he might have a late vocation to the priesthood. Joe considers it, and then spends almost two weeks of his vacation working with the homeless at a Catholic Worker house. He develops a rededication to the gospel. When he returns home, he accepts an appointment to a new parish whose name is revealing: Holy Cross. Joe Hackett rediscovers his vocation through a rediscovery of Christ's cross and resurrection as the heart of the gospel. He rediscovers a calling to bear witness to what God has done and is doing in the world by the power of the Holy Spirit.

That is to say, there is hope even for those mired in mud. The title of the novel, *Wheat That Springeth Green*, is taken from a hymn whose allu-

22. Powers, *Wheat That Springeth Green*, p. 200.
23. Powers, *Wheat That Springeth Green*, pp. 327-28.

sions go back to John 12:24.[24] The hymn suggests that love returns "that with the dead has been," just as the wheat "that in dark earth many days has lain" comes back to life as a "green blade." The hymn serves as a reminder that even in the midst of spirals downward, of conceptions and practices of ministry that are mired in mud, there is hope for a resurrected commitment to the life-giving character of ordained ministry lived faithfully and well. So also there is hope for resurrecting excellence, a commitment to the practices and holy friendships that nurture Christian discipleship and the journey to the "everlasting holy places."

Office and Its Distortion into Hierarchy and Bureaucracy

There are perennial tensions in the church about how best to understand the exemplary role of those set aside to serve as pastoral leaders in relation to the centrality of the exemplary role of Jesus Christ. These tensions are heightened by questions about who has authority to do what, and who is permitted to exercise power in the community. There is warrant for concern, especially given Jesus' warnings about those who seek power, who seek to be first, and his injunctions that we should not seek to be lords but rather servants (see Mark 8–10, especially 8:34-35; 9:35; 10:43-45).

The problem, of course, is that leadership of any organization offers seductions of power, prestige, and flattery. This becomes especially tempting for clergy, who can cloak abuses of their power in religious language about being servants. Yet there are resources to check temptations to self-glorifying power, to selfish ambition: we have the calling to humility found in service, to lives that are patterned in the dying and rising of Christ. This calling is, and ought to be, heightened for the clergy, who are called to exemplary lives of holiness as an encouraging focus for all Christians.

As we will suggest in the next chapter, this does not mean that Christians should avoid the use of power. Power will be exercised; the question is whether we have ways to exercise it faithfully. We need to cultivate the wise use of power, the faithful wisdom of governance, in

24. "Now the Green Blade Riseth," words by John M. C. Crum (1872-1958); music, *Noël Nouvelet*, medieval French carol.

Christian life and Christian ministry as an exemplary means for its wise use in other vocations.

Over the course of Christian history, various movements have emerged that, out of either an authentic but naïve desire for faithful service or a reaction to abusive power, have sought to sustain Christian community without any sense of a set-aside ministry. But that has not resolved the problem with power and the ordering of the community. As Richard John Neuhaus notes, "The community is still left with differences of gifts (*charismata*) and functions, and if these are not to be exercised in an arbitrary and tyrannical way, they must be regularized and held accountable to the community in clearly designated offices. Thus we have the irony that office, which has so often been the source of authoritarianism, is also essential to freedom."[25] The office of pastoral ministry is focused as a representation of Christ, and so provides a pattern by which pastoral leadership should be articulated and accountability measured. The clergy are not expected to be Christ, but they are expected to exercise leadership in a manner consistent with Christ. That is at the heart of resurrecting excellence.[26]

Gifts for Pastoral Leadership

How do we faithfully discern gifts for pastoral leadership? Human beings yearn to discover gifts and talents that enable us to make a contribution to the world in which we live. We long to have our hearts, convictions, and passions aligned with our gifts and talents, an alignment that creates beauty and signifies that we are in communion with the Triune God and moving toward the "everlasting holy places." But such alignment is very difficult to discern in a world marked by sin manifested in self-deception, fragmentation, and other forms of brokenness. In such a world, the simple question

25. Neuhaus, *Freedom for Ministry*, p. 205.

26. Neuhaus insightfully notes: "[T]he pursuit of holiness is premised upon the belief, indeed the Divine promise, that there is a complementarity of excellences. The vocation of each member is unique, and each member should sustain all other members in discerning and pursuing their peculiar callings. Conflicts arise only when people try to pursue vocations that belong to somebody else." *Freedom for Ministry*, p. 207.

"Who Am I?" is fraught with uncertainty and tension — even to the point of recognizing that "I" may not be the best interpreter of my own particular gifts.

This insight is powerfully displayed in Dietrich Bonhoeffer's poem "Who Am I?" Written while he was in prison toward the end of World War II for his work in helping Jews escape the horrors of Hitler's reign, Bonhoeffer's question is haunted by the possibility that others may know him better than he knows himself — but that only God really knows him fully.

Who Am I?

Who am I? They often tell me
I would step from my cell's confinement
calmly, cheerfully, firmly,
like a squire from his country-house.

Who am I? They often tell me
I would talk to my warders
freely and friendly and clearly
as though it were mine to command.

Who am I? They also tell me
I would bear the days of misfortune
equably, smilingly, proudly,
like one accustomed to win.

Am I really all that which other men tell of?
Or am I only what I know of myself,
restless and longing and sick, like a bird in a cage,
struggling for breath, as though hands were compressing my
    throat,
yearning for colours, for flowers, for the voices of birds,
thirsting for words of kindness, for neighbourliness,
trembling with anger at despotisms and petty humiliation,
tossing in expectation of great events,
powerlessly trembling for friends at an infinite distance,
weary and empty at praying, at thinking, at making,
faint, and ready to say farewell to it all?

Who am I? This or the other?
Am I one person today, and tomorrow another?
Am I both at once? A hypocrite before others,
and before myself a contemptibly woebegone weakling?
Or is something within me still like a beaten army,
Fleeing in disorder from victory already achieved?

Who am I? They mock me, these lonely questions of mine.
Whoever I am, thou knowest, O God, I am thine.[27]

Bonhoeffer recognizes that his own self-perception may be at odds with the truth about himself. His own self-understanding, beaten down by interrogation and isolation, may have created in himself a "beaten army" that is now "fleeing in disorder from victory already achieved."

Conversely, at other times, and for other people, the problem may be that one's self-perception is excessively self-glorifying. In such circumstances, the problem is that I see myself in ways that diminish and destroy others precisely by my assertion of a distorted and distorting deployment of power.

Contexts, histories, and temperaments play an enormously significant role in shaping our complex senses of ourselves. As Bonhoeffer's example shows, someone who suffers under oppression typically struggles with a lack of a sense of self, whereas those in power tend to reinforce their own images of dominance and self-assertion. Moreover, some people are temperamentally prone to excessive self-preoccupation and self-criticism, whereas others seem oblivious to their own distortions or failings.

We human beings tend to be a complicated mixture of self-assertion and self-abnegation, caught in webs of self-deception of which we are unaware. So also do we tend to fail to discern accurately our own gifts and calling. We often get the discernment partially right, but also partially wrong. Over time, we seek to learn how to narrate our lives truthfully in ways that will enable us to discover the life that really is life.

We do so by locating our lives, as Bonhoeffer does at the end of

27. Dietrich Bonhoeffer, *Letters and Papers from Prison*, trans. Eberhard Bethge (1953; New York: Simon & Schuster, 1997), pp. 347-48.

his poem, in relation to God. Only God knows fully who we are. As we seek to identify how God is calling us to live by patterning our lives in the life, death, and resurrection of Christ, we discover how the particular, distinctive story of each of our lives can be returned to us redemptively. We find this truth in and through the practices and friendships of Christian community; and as we grow in grace and truth in our own lives, we become more faithful carriers of the conviction that redemptive truthfulness is revealed in Christ for the sake of the world for each of us as persons. In receiving the gift of calling from Christ, we also thereby become agents of hope and beauty — for bearing witness that there are, indeed, "everlasting holy places" for all God's children.

Hence, Christian congregations have an essential ministry both in embodying a distinctive vocation to the life found in Jesus Christ and in creating hospitable spaces for people to discern by the power of the Holy Spirit their own distinctive and personal vocations in following Jesus. These hospitable spaces are found in covenant groups and other holy friendships within congregations, as well as spiritual renewal programs such as Cursillo or Walk to Emmaus that work across congregations.

Some churches are well known for helping their members discern the diverse vocations to which they are being called. These congregations cultivate various networks of relationships and, especially, holy friendships in which people find accountability, support, and encouragement to dream as they discern how to live ever more deeply into their baptism. One pastor has developed a practice of writing notes to the young teenagers in his congregation, telling them that he has been paying attention to how God is at work in their lives and inviting them to lunch to discuss their vocations. Is it any wonder that this congregation sends a number of young people into ordained ministry, as well as intentionally Christian practices of medicine, law, business, education, and social work?

The church is called to foster the ministry of all Christians in their life in the world. As Richard John Neuhaus provocatively notes, "The vocation of the Church is to sustain many vocations." What, then, is the particular calling of those who are asked to provide pastoral leadership by being ordained? Neuhaus continues: "The ordained minister, the one set aside and consecrated, is to illuminate the vocation of the Church and the vocations of the many people who are the Church. That means that ordination is not exclusionary but exemplary."[28]

Too often, especially in our contemporary climate of "experts," people who have had a profound Christian awakening (whether through conversion or a deepening of faith already confessed) assume that the only way to express the seriousness of that commitment is to become ordained. Some may be experiencing a genuine calling to pastoral leadership, but others often need help in seeing that their awakening may be expressed more faithfully through their vocations in the world.

There is indeed a "special" calling for those who are to become pastoral leaders. It is often a complex set of gifts, experiences, and developing intimacy with God that shines forth in a person's own sense of God's direction. In a way similar to a person's discernment that she is called to become a Christian physician, or another's discernment that he is called to become a faithful musician, so those called to become ordained clergy discern a sense that God is leading them into a special, exemplary vocation of pastoral ministry. This is what Niebuhr calls the "secret" call.

Yet that secret call needs to be confirmed by the providential and ecclesiastical dimensions of the calling, the sense that there is a good fit between a person's gifts and what the church needs from its pastoral leaders. That is, people do not set *themselves* aside for pastoral leadership. The church calls people who have the gifts, and the potential capacities, to provide the skills, learning, and wisdom that the church needs to flourish and to enable the flourishing of its members.

The fundamental capacities and gifts for pastoral leadership can be profitably limned in terms of the three dimensions of the pastoral vocation — calling, profession, and office. Each dimension requires a particular giftedness for its faithful fulfillment. At the same time, just as the richest conceptions of the pastoral vocation are found in the mutual complementarity of the three dimensions, the richest practices of pastoral ministry are found in the vital synergies of their capacities and gifts.

We suggest that essential to the dimension of calling is the gift of attentiveness; essential to profession, the gift of practical wisdom; and essential to office, the gift of administration. These associations are by no means exclusive; nor are they exhaustive. Indeed, their intersections and generative spirals will be apparent even in our brief descrip-

28. Neuhaus, *Freedom for Ministry*, p. 203.

tions. But we believe that they can provide a helpful basis for understanding the rich complex of capacities and gifts through which we build up the community of Christ and strengthen its witness.

Calling and the Gift of Attentiveness

The church appropriately expects that those who are entrusted with the vessels of the Lord are committed to reliance on a faithful way of life, discerning clearly both their own calling as Christians and their particular calling to serve as pastoral leaders. They must have a capacity for listening attentively, both to God and to others — a skill that is rarer than we sometimes assume. Indeed, fidelity to a vocation, whether lay or ordained, is fundamentally a lifelong task of listening attentively and obediently to the prompting of God's Holy Spirit.

Those entrusted with leadership need to be particularly attentive in listening — to Scripture, to the community, to the needs of others, to the ways of God in the world. Too often we speak before we have listened, directly contrary to the injunction of James 1:19 to "be quick to listen, slow to speak, slow to anger." Our capacity to listen, to pay attention, is essential to excellence in our calling.

The philosopher Simone Weil writes powerfully about the critical role of attentiveness for the spiritual life. Our colleague Stephanie Paulsell drew our attention to Weil's thought and its relation to the intellectual work of ministry:

> I love to read Simone Weil's essay "On the Right Use of School Studies with a View to the Love of God" with students just beginning their preparation for ministry. In that essay, Weil insists that academic study is a pearl of great price, worthy of the sacrifice of our time and resources to pursue, because it can prepare us for a more profound engagement with God and others. She makes this argument not by emphasizing the content of what we must know, but rather the capacity we must cultivate in order to be able to pray or to be present to our suffering neighbor. That capacity, the capacity for attention, can be developed through intellectual work, she argues, because such work demands that we make ourselves patiently available to what is other than ourselves. When we develop

the capacity to be attentive to grammars and ideas and vocabularies that are not our own, she insists, our capacity to pray and to be present to those who are suffering increases.

. . . My hope for these students is that they come to understand the academic work they are called upon to do in divinity school not as . . . a necessary interruption on the way to the real work of ministry, but as an immersion in a set of practices that will shape their souls and teach them the attentive stance towards all of life which undergirds excellent ministry.[29]

Profession and the Gift of Practical Wisdom

We appropriately expect that pastoral leaders will have natural and acquired capacities conducive to practical wisdom — a capacity for rigorous study of Scripture and other classical and contemporary texts, as well as a capacity for guiding processes of practical reasoning among the whole people of God.

Pastoral leaders are called to be wise preachers and teachers of the gospel, proclaiming the gospel in word and deed. This is emphasized particularly in Protestant traditions, but it is a vital task for any gathered community both internally and in evangelistic settings. Paul asks in reference to finding salvation by calling on the name of the Lord, "But how are they to call on one in whom they have not believed? And how are they to believe in one of whom they have never heard? And how are they to hear without someone to proclaim him? And how are they to proclaim him unless they are sent? As it is written, 'How beautiful are the feet of those who bring good news!'" (Rom. 10:14-15). Faithful, deep, and wise preaching is longed for by mature disciples as well as seekers, those who have dwelt with the Scriptures day by day in faithful study and practice as well as those who have come to church for the first time out of curiosity.

29. Stephanie Paulsell, "Excellence in Ministry and the Practice of Reading" (Colloquium on Excellence in Ministry, Duke Divinity School, Durham, NC, May 16-17, 2002), pp. 2-3. A version of this essay appears as "'The Inscribed Heart: A Spirituality of Intellectual Work': Reading as a Spiritual Practice," in *Lexington Theological Quarterly* 36 (Fall 2001): 139-54. Simone Weil's essay is in Weil, *Waiting for God*, trans. Emma Craufurd (New York: Putnam, 1951), pp. 105-16.

The great African American writer James Weldon Johnson beautifully and poetically illumines the stakes for the preacher in the third
stanza of his poem "Listen, Lord — A Prayer":

> And now, O Lord, this man of God,
> Who breaks the bread of life this morning —
> Shadow him in the hollow of thy hand,
> And keep him out of the gunshot of the devil.
> Take him, Lord — this morning —
> Wash him with hyssop inside and out,
> Hang him up and drain him dry of sin.
> Pin his ear to the wisdom-post,
> And make his words sledge hammers of truth —
> Beating on the iron heart of sin.
> Lord God, this morning —
> Put his eye to the telescope of eternity,
> And let him look upon the paper walls of time.
> Lord, turpentine his imagination,
> Put perpetual motion in his arms,
> Fill him full of the dynamite of thy power,
> Anoint him all over with the oil of thy Salvation,
> And set his tongue on fire.[30]

The preacher is expected to break the bread of life for the congregation through her words, utterly dependent on God, yet also in need of
connecting to the "wisdom-post"; capable of seeing eternity through a
telescope, yet with a tongue on fire to testify to the dynamite of God's
power in the here and now. A daunting vision, indeed — but also one
in which God capacitates those who are called to preach through their
natural gifts, acquired talents, lifelong study, and ongoing learning of
faithful discipleship in friendship with God.

The clergy are also called to be teachers of the gospel. Jesus' Great
Commission in Matthew 28 calls his followers to go into the world
and make disciples of all nations, baptizing them in the name of the

30. James Weldon Johnson, "Listen, Lord — A Prayer," from *God's Trombones*
(New York: Viking, 1927; reissue, New York: Penguin, 1990), p. 14, cited in Richard
Lischer, ed., *The Company of Preachers* (Grand Rapids: Eerdmans, 2002), pp. xvii-xviii.

Father, Son, and Holy Spirit, and *teaching* them to obey all that Jesus had commanded them. Those called to pastoral leadership need to claim an identity as teachers throughout their ministry, to reclaim a sense of lifelong learning for themselves and all disciples. This includes a more robust catechetical process at the beginning of the Christian journey, and also a sense of the ongoing need for mentors and apprentices at every step of the way. This is because all disciples, pastors and laity alike, are joint inquirers seeking to learn from Christ who is, as Augustine notes, the "true teacher," who made the cross his professorial chair.[31] Stephanie Paulsell observed this crucial commitment to joint inquiry at work in one of her students:

> I am sitting in my office when Santiago Pinon, a first-year M.Div. student, comes to tell me of his excitement over a class he is taking on negative theology with Jean-Luc Marion and David Tracy. He is holding in his hands a copy of Professor Marion's book *God Without Being*. As he pages through it, looking for his favorite passages, I can see that Santiago has marked up the book in at least three colors of ink.
>
> "The first time I read this book," Santiago says, "I read every sentence three times, just trying to figure out what Professor Marion was saying. Now," he says, "I am reading it again, trying to figure out what the idea of a God without being might have to say to the homeless ex-convicts I work with. I think there is something here for them."
>
> He was reading it again, not just through his own eyes, but through the eyes of formerly incarcerated, badly wounded men. And he expected to find something for them there.
>
> For those of us who are wondering why we should keep reading when the world is falling apart, this is one important answer. This is a way of reading on behalf of the world. . . . Santiago made himself available to *others* as he did the hard work of reading and rereading, outlining and underlining that the text required.

Every minister needs to know how to do this, how to read on behalf of others. Tom Long says this is precisely the work of the preacher. In *The Witness of Preaching*, he says that the preacher goes to

---

31. Augustine, *Sermon* 234.2, cited in William Harmless, *Augustine and the Catechumenate* (Collegeville, Minn.: Liturgical Press, 1995), p. 326.

the text on behalf of the people. The reading and study that preaching requires is not preparation for ministry, he insists; it *is* ministry.[32]

The challenge of having pastoral leaders who are gifted preachers and teachers is not simply that they become educated or learned. Rather, it is that they have the capacity, the eyes to see and ears to hear and mouths to speak, to discern the work of God in the world. This involves careful study of doctrine, ongoing learning from those before us and those around us, and a capacity to translate learning into wisdom that is communicated in diverse settings with diverse people. As we will suggest in the next chapter, this has more to do with a commitment to "learning ministry" throughout life than with the more passive sense of a "learned minister."

Office and the Gift of Administration

The church ought also to expect that the clergy will manifest the holiness appropriate to the pastoral office, and a capacity to see how administration is integral to the life of ministry — even as it is important to remember that the church's faithfulness does not depend on the holiness of the clergy or the effectiveness of their administrative work. There should be signs of growth in holy living and administration over time, even as we acknowledge that a new pastor will typically be marked more by potential than by the fullness of a holy life or the gifts of administrative leadership

There has been a tendency to downplay the administrative aspects of ordained ministry because of our ambivalence about power and authority, or perhaps to rebel against them because of the ways in which management theories and bureaucratic expectations have afflicted the contemporary church's self-understanding. However, the root for the term "administration" is the same word as for "ministry," and the question is not whether pastors will provide administrative leadership — it is whether it will be done well or poorly. Richard Lischer offers a compelling theological account:

32. Paulsell, "Excellence in Ministry," pp. 15-17. The reference to Long is from *The Witness of Preaching* (Louisville: Westminster John Knox, 1989), pp. 44-45.

Administration, so despised by the high-minded and neglected by the seminaries, takes on real meaning when it is understood as an extension of the most important administrative work of all, the administration of the sacraments. The unproductive hours and busy work that all pastors complain of can be traced to the broken connection between administration as a secular tool and the administration of word and sacraments as a spiritual discipline. Pastoral administration, or stewardship, begins with stewardship of God's mysteries.[33]

Why is administrative leadership, an important aspect of pastoral leadership at any time, so critically important in our contemporary context? We live in a time of ecclesial and cultural transition and even upheaval, a time when it is challenging to discern how to sustain as well as renovate institutions, how to heal and grow communities that are being ruptured by divisions, and to find innovative forms for building new institutions while allowing decaying ones to die.[34]

Gregory the Great, whose *Pastoral Care* was written in part to explain why he thought he was not called to be pope (his argument obviously failed), showed remarkable innovation and traditioned faithfulness as an administrative leader. The challenges of administrative leadership are different in small and large congregations, and they are quite complex for large institutions that directly and indirectly serve the church's proclamation and embodiment of the gospel. The commonality is that, in whatever situations pastoral leaders are called to serve, they need to nurture gifts of administrative leadership for the sake of the church's fidelity, creativity, and excellence.

*   *   *

The vocation to pastoral leadership is costly for those who undertake it. It is not a job that can easily be put down, nor should it be a role

33. Richard Lischer, "The Called Life: An Essay on the Pastoral Vocation," *Interpretation* 59 (2005): 173.

34. For an excellent example of the transformative potential of wise pastoral leadership in the area of administration, see Bishop Claude E. Payne and Hamilton Beazley, *Reclaiming the Great Commission* (San Francisco: Jossey-Bass, 2000). Their faithfulness and innovation enabled effective ministry to be enhanced in a situation of significant cultural and ecclesial change.

that involves masks that are put on and taken off. It is a vocation that is intrinsically bound up with the shaping of character, a calling to a particular way of life. It is a profession with high standards of competence and performance. It is an office that expects a lot of those who occupy it, even as it also offers fulfillment and satisfaction. The demands are great, the list of requisite skills is daunting, and the earthly remuneration is comparatively small (even if, and when, the economic challenges of ministry are more adequately addressed than they have been in recent decades). It is also a vocation, as we have already suggested, in which success is not always easy to measure.

In addition, the vocation asks clergy to provide courage in calling the community to bear appropriate witness to the gospel, faithful interpretation in preaching and teaching, and exemplary holiness. The clergy are asked to go and serve where they are needed most, to distinguish what is important from what is urgent, and to develop agility to be able to address people's needs in ways that stretch the clergy's own dispositions and gifts. There is no escaping the fact that being a pastor is a demanding and costly vocation, even appropriately understood and lived. The eighteenth-century clergyman and hymn writer John Newton described being a pastor as at one and the same time "the worst of all jobs and the best of all callings."

The fact that it is the best of all callings suggests that, even amid the costs, there is also the potential for an extraordinary fitness between those called to ordained ministry and the life to be lived. The calling to pastoral ministry is undergirded and sustained by God's grace and the promise that God will embrace, sustain, and support those set aside for it. In addition, there are wonderful gifts to be found in administering the sacraments and being welcomed into the holy moments of people's lives — presiding at weddings, rejoicing in the births of babies, participating with the Spirit as lives are turned around through conversion, witnessing growth in discipleship, engaging together in practices of justice and reconciliation, sharing the poignancy of illnesses faced and the sanctity of the end of life.

Yet there also needs to be a creative tension in the fitness between ordained clergy and those they are called to serve. Often ministry is most holy, and congregations most faithfully challenged, when both the pastor and the congregation are called to stretch their gifts in order to relate to each other. Too close a fit can mean too much comfort.

So, for example, a young pastor named Roy Terry, who wears his hair in a ponytail, is most comfortable in blue jeans and a clerical collar, loves praise bands as well as hymns like "Lift High the Cross," and celebrates every-Sunday Eucharist, was sent to start a new congregation in Naples, Florida. He describes his style of worship as "radical liturgical." It might seem strange for such a pastor to begin a new church in a community with large numbers of retirees. But he has sought to nurture a congregation that welcomes retirees as well as young seekers, wealthy businesspeople as well as immigrant blue-collar workers, people of diverse ethnic backgrounds, and weave them into a faith-filled, excellent congregation.

It seems clear that this is a congregation whose ministries are beautiful and filled with ambition for the gospel, in which the fit-ness of clergy and congregation has had to be worked at rather than presumed. Yet this also points to the wonderful capacity for God's surprises to be manifest in resurrecting excellence in ministry. When you think about ways in which things could go wrong, this new church seems like a recipe for disaster. Yet it has flourished, largely because the people who gather as the church are convinced that the gospel matters, their lives are centered in God, and they have a pastor whose way of life is genuinely focused on drawing the souls of his neighbors to the "everlasting holy places." The life of this pastor and this congregation reveal a vocation for the church that sustains the many vocations of its members, and it is led by a pastor who recognizes the rich theological interplay of calling, profession, and office. Their life together holds surprises for many, and yet in those surprises they are discovering life transformed, the life that really is life — a beautiful ministry of resurrecting excellence.

How, then, do we cultivate pastoral leaders who will both embody excellence in their own vocations and inspire excellence among their congregations, institutions, and the particular people with whom they are in ministry? We believe that we need to pay more attention to the ongoing tasks of learning pastoral ministry over a lifetime, and especially what such attention will entail for shaping faithful Christian communities and leading institutions in this time of cultural transition and uncertainty. It is to these matters that we turn in the next chapter.

5 Learning and Leading: The Cultivation of Excellent Ministry

Christianity in the United States, especially Protestant Christianity, has long upheld an ideal of a "learned clergy." This ideal has been built partly on the image of the pastor as a professional, but it is rooted also in an emphasis on the pastor as preacher and teacher. Many of the earliest colleges and universities were founded in order to cultivate a learned clergy. The founders of Harvard College, for example, sought to avoid leaving "an illiterate Ministry to the Churches, when our present ministers shall lie in the Dust."[1] Many colleges first pursued this mission in undergraduate studies in the arts and sciences; indeed, the same education was understood to fit one for service in either church or state. When the time came that the colleges felt a need for more focused studies for future clergy, they endowed professorships of divinity, formed departments around them, and eventually established the divinity schools whose work it was, and is, to create a learned clergy for the church.

This understanding of a learned clergy has had a profound impact on our conceptions of ministry. It is a vision of the clergy's vocation that is deeply engaged with tasks of preaching and teaching as well as with public issues, questions, and concerns. There is much to commend the image that it conveys, an image of a professional who is learned and able to offer understanding and insight to congregations as well as the wider society.

1. The quotation is from a 1643 pamphlet entitled *New England's First Fruits* by Harvard College president Henry Dunster.

Even so, there are significant limits to the image. It seems difficult to connect the notion of a "learned clergy" with an emphasis on calling or office, especially a sense of the importance of cultivating a holy life. They are not incompatible, but on a "learned clergy" model, education seems to displace a concern with either calling and spiritual formation or office and holiness. Indeed, one of the criticisms of the "professional" model of clergy is that it is preoccupied with "book learning" rather than calling and relationship with God. The phrase "learned clergy" does not seem to evoke a call to a life marked by rigorous and loving attention to God and those with whom the pastor is in ministry, a life that turns toward the world and its joy as well as its sorrow.

Too often the phrase "learned clergy" evokes the image of George Eliot's Mr. Casaubon in *Middlemarch:* a man in his library, barricaded from human life by his manuscripts, wholly consumed by a scholarly project that will never bear fruit in the world. Or the image evokes the "gentleman" whom John Henry Newman criticizes in *The Idea of a University,* a person who is cultured, but not changed, by his studies.

The image of the learned clergy is also often associated with an elitist set of assumptions, in which the clergy are elevated above and apart from the ordinary lives of parishioners and other laity in the world. It conveys a sense of someone with specialized knowledge that is fundamentally distinct from that of others, thus entitling the clergy to a privileged place — in the community, and often, assumed to be privileged in relation to God. With this loss of focus on how God calls all people to ministry, and then sets aside some to provide pastoral leadership, the ordering of ministry goes awry.

We do not propose getting rid of the image of the learned clergy entirely, however. It is an image with a long, rich history in which we ourselves stand, and, indeed, we believe it is important to emphasize the intellectual dimensions of pastoral ministry. Like any vocation, intellectual work can be done well or poorly; it can form or deform. And it is important that the education and formation of clergy offer a spacious vision for a critical, lively, and generous-spirited intellectual life as an integral feature of the pastoral vocation.

We believe that we can retain the strengths of the image of a "learned clergy," and overcome its weaknesses, if we modify the phrase slightly — to "learning clergy." We suggest that learning is a lifelong vocation: one that begins with learning to feel and think and act as a disciple of Jesus Christ, that continues through formal educative formation to become a pastor, and then continues with learning throughout pastoral ministry as one preaches, celebrates the sacraments, leads, and equips others to learn and grow in their own vocations as disciples. Our image depends on the recognition that "learning" involves the shaping of our hearts as well as our minds and hands and feet, the cultivation of a way of life that is affective, cognitive, disciplined, and integrally connected to action.

Spiritual Formation: Life in the Fountain of God's Love

The faithful and effective cultivation of "learning clergy" depends, in its formative phases, on the faithful and effective commitment to learning for all disciples of Jesus Christ. This is integral to our description in Chapter 3 of the calling to Christian ministry for all people. All Christians need to be shaped to love God with their hearts, souls, minds, and strength.

Saint Catherine of Siena suggests that we do this by locating our lives in the fountain of God's love. Friendship, the Father tells her in *The Dialogue*, "is just like a vessel that you fill at the fountain. If you take it out of the fountain to drink, the vessel is soon empty. But if you hold your vessel in the fountain while you drink, it will not get empty: Indeed, it will always be full. So the love of your neighbor, whether spiritual or temporal, is meant to be drunk in me, without any self-interest."[2] As Suzanne Noffke summarizes Catherine's view, the fountain is "the heart of Christ, and the love that we drink in perfect friendship is his blood, the fire of charity, the Holy Spirit of God."[3]

Apart from that fountain, apart from the love that is the fire of charity, the Holy Spirit of God, our lives become empty. By so locating our lives in that fountain, we will be continually refreshed and nourished by the self-giving love of the Trinity. How do we do so? By nurturing faithful habits of learning through ongoing disciplined prac-

2. Catherine of Siena, *The Dialogue*, trans. Suzanne Noffke, O.P. (New York: Paulist, 1980), 64, p. 121.

3. Suzanne Noffke, O.P., *Catherine of Siena* (Collegeville, Minn.: Liturgical Press, 1996), p. 36.

tices and holy friendships that are centered in God and directed toward the goal of life with God in the kingdom.

The first step in cultivating a "learning clergy" focuses on the kind of learning that all disciples need as a part of their initiation into a Christian way of life. It is important to develop patterns of catechesis, the process by which people become Christians through confirmation or adult baptism, that are attentive to the comprehensive shape of learning to feel, think, and act as Christians. The Roman Catholic "Rite of Christian Initiation of Adults" is instructive in this regard, especially in the way it draws on insights from ancient practices of catechesis that were more robust and comprehensive than modern practices tend to be.[4] Indeed, one of the problems of training contemporary clergy is that formal education often has to do so much "remedial catechesis" that it is unable to do the work it is actually best equipped to do. One of our seminary classmates, upon learning in his second year of study that he had been assigned a text from the Letter to the Hebrews for his next sermon in preaching class, remarked without irony: "Darn it! I wanted a New Testament text." When there is a lack of emphasis on learning discipleship for all Christians, and formal education must do remedial catechesis, the result is discouraging: the clergy are often not only less "learned" than the image of a learned clergy would suggest but also less well formed as faithful disciples of Jesus Christ than a deep and rich sense of calling and office should expect.[5]

Good patterns of catechesis immerse people in Scripture, orienting all Christians to a way of life in which Scripture becomes "a word that journeys with us."[6] This way of life in turn nurtures a scriptural

4. See the discussion of the significance of ancient catechesis in L. Gregory Jones, "Baptism," in *Knowing the Triune God*, ed. James J. Buckley and David S. Yeago (Grand Rapids: Eerdmans, 2001), pp. 147-78.

5. This is indeed a perpetual, not just a contemporary, problem. We do not intend to invoke nostalgia for a nonexistent past when all of the clergy were well formed and well educated. The claim that the clergy are ill formed and ill educated is a recurrent, in fact persistent, theme in each generation — especially in American culture. But our point is that contemporary practices and structures have exacerbated the perpetual problem, presenting the church with distinctive challenges as well as opportunities.

6. We take the notion of Scripture as a "word that journeys with us" from Hans Urs von Balthasar. See his *Theo-Drama*, vol. 2, trans. Graham Harrison (San Francisco: Ignatius, 1990), pp. 102ff. See also the discussion in L. Gregory Jones, "The Word That Journeys With Us," *Theology Today* 55 (April 1998): 69-76.

imagination, helping us faithfully interpret Scripture's significance for our lives. Further, good catechesis teaches us the content of the Lord's Prayer as well as the Creed, helping us discover doctrine as a practice that is life-giving both in conveying content and in shaping a faithful understanding of, and relationship with, God.

Christians are called to be people for whom the language of Scripture becomes a "second first language," so that we read the world, and our lives, through the lens of Scripture. Our colleague Willie James Jennings notes that Scripture was so central in his family and his church as he was growing up that it took him a long time to discover that "Ruth, Naomi, Paul, and even Jesus, weren't part of the extended family." Of course, in a very real sense they *are* a part of the extended family.

Christian life sets us on a journey of learning to have eyes to see and ears to hear God's work in the world. We need attentiveness to prayer, Scripture, Christian doctrine, and spiritual direction that can orient us toward friendship with God and cultivate right beliefs that will shape our practical reasoning. We also need to engage in the ongoing practices of Christian life that are the sustenance of Christian congregations. And we need to engage in those practices of discipleship in the world that illumine our life in Christ.

We do so by learning these practices together and, especially as we are being initiated into Christian faith, by apprenticing ourselves to those who are wise. Like Southport Church's confirmation class, we need to see how Christian life is learned and lived over time in the company of others, especially those who are wiser than we are and farther along the journey of faithful living. Such learning of the practices of discipleship is an ongoing task, embracing the youngest of children to the oldest of adults, laity as well as clergy, those who are succeeding at the heights of their vocations as well as those who are struggling to discern who they are and to have a vocation at all. Christian life involves lifelong learning.

This lifelong learning includes both formative and critical inquiry, and while it is primarily located in congregations, it includes relationships with formal institutions as well as settings of social engagement. Those who have learned to see and hear God's work in the world will be able to draw significant analogies between their Christian faith and their day-to-day vocations and lives. So, for example, ordinary faithful Christians have initiated and sustained ministries through houses of hospitality, hospice communities, L'Arche communities for the developmentally disabled, and other settings that bear witness to the dignity of human life not predicated on a person's productivity. Similarly, guilds of Christian physicians have focused on shaping their vocations in the light of their Christian convictions, leading to renewed emphases on healing and care as well as service to those in underserved areas. And Christians in South Africa, during the most difficult days of the struggle against apartheid, found themselves drawn to participate in the drama of Holy Week, and especially Good Friday, because it articulated the power of their struggle and suffering.

Learning is central throughout our lives as Christian disciples. So it is not surprising to find that St. Ambrose, in his fourth-century treatise on the duties of the clergy, emphasizes the shaping of character through discipleship and apprenticeship as a crucial prerequisite for shaping faithful clergy. He stresses that we learn Christian life in the first instance by turning to those wise people who can serve as a "mirror of virtue." The primary reference is to Christ, and then to those people who are exemplars and exhorters in Scripture. Ambrose notes that "the word of God should come down upon us like the dew." He suggests that this immersion in Christ and biblical exemplars is significantly enhanced by an ongoing process of training and practice in friendship with faithful and wise Christians.[7]

When Ambrose turns to the particular duties of the clergy, he builds on this foundation: "And I am speaking of the duties which I wish to impress upon and impart to you, whom I have chosen for the service of the Lord; so that those things which have been already implanted and fixed in your minds and characters by habit and training may now be further unfolded to you by explanation and instruction."[8]

Ambrose stresses that those who are set aside to lead others must be people of excellent character themselves. He notes: "Such, then, ought he to be who gives counsel to another, in order that he

---

7. Ambrose, *De officiis ministrorum*, in *Nicene and Post-Nicene Fathers*, second series, vol. 10 (New York: Christian Literature, 1896), pp. 1-89. The particular quotations are found at 1.25.116, p. 20 and 1.32.165, p. 28.

8. Ambrose, *De officiis ministrorum* 2.6.25, p. 47.

may offer himself as a pattern in all good works, in teaching, in true-ness of character, in seriousness. Thus his words will be wholesome and irreproachable, his counsel useful, his life virtuous, and his opin-ions seemly. . . . He must have nothing dark, or deceptive, or false about him, to cast a shadow on his life and character, nothing wicked or evil to keep back those who want advice." Or, in more earthy terms: "Who seeks for a spring in the mud? Who wants to drink from muddy water?"[9]

Gregory the Great, like Ambrose, believes that the first step to-ward the cultivation of a "learning clergy" is formation in the faithful practices of Christian discipleship. Gregory, too, stresses the impor-tance of character, and character's role in the development of wisdom and discernment for preaching and teaching and counseling others. Gregory's description of pastoral leadership as "the art of arts" is predicated on the claim of Gregory of Nazianzus in the fourth century that "to rule men is the art of arts, and the science of sciences, for man is a being of diversity and manifold character." Gregory the Great takes this rather clinical view of human complexity and casts it in a more pastoral key: "The government of souls," he writes, "is the art of arts. For who does not realize that the wounds of the mind are more hidden than the internal wounds of the body?"[10]

It is not accidental, we believe, that both Ambrose in the fourth century and Gregory in the sixth would emphasize the importance of the clergy's capacity for wisdom and character, and the agility that ac-companies them. For both lived in times of significant transition in which issues of leadership, governance, and the building and shaping of institutions loomed particularly large. In both their writing and as exemplars, they display what it means to keep learning throughout life in the contexts of preaching and teaching as well as leadership and governance.

In our time, those who are called and set aside to become clergy need similar patterns of explanation and instruction. There remains a central role for the kind of formal education and disciplined learning

---

9. Ambrose, *De officiis ministrorum* 2.17.86, 88, p. 57; 2.12.60, p. 52.

10. Gregory Nazianzus, *Orations* 2.16, cited in note 1 to part 1 in Gregory the Great, *Pastoral Care*, trans. Henry Davis, S.J. (New York: Newman, 1950), p. 242. Gregory the Great's quotation is from *Pastoral Care* 1.1, p. 21.

that help shape appropriate character and cultivate wisdom and discernment. In addition, the clergy need to be encouraged to see what it means to be exemplary administrators, focused on the Christian practice of shaping communities and leading institutions. For, as we have been suggesting throughout this book, we live in a time in which we face significant challenges and remarkable opportunities for creating, renovating, sustaining, and extending Christian communities and Christian institutions.

Hence, we turn next to the question of the kind of education that is needed for those who are set aside to become clergy, and then to the question of cultivating leadership and governance as a Christian practice.

Education: Cultivating a Pastoral and Ecclesial Imagination

What kind of theological education is needed for those who are to become clergy, and in what settings? For several centuries in the West, and especially in the United States, an influential presumption has been that we need institutions of formal theological education to prepare people for Christian ministry. This has been grounded in the professional model, and has presumed that such institutions will provide explanation and instruction that builds on the catechesis people have received in and through congregations. While not all traditions have required such formal education, this model became increasingly predominant during the twentieth century.

There is much to commend formal theological education, and we believe it is indispensable for cultivating the kind of knowledge, wisdom, and character that the clergy need to flourish in their vocations. However, the conventional model by which a "learned clergy" was supposed to be formed has broken down, and the church and academy have developed a mutual suspicion and even hostility rather than the synergy that is critical for shaping the clergy to be people who learn throughout their vocations.

At root, there are at least two problems with the conventional model of a "relay race," in which congregations form people for ministry and then pass them on to seminaries for critical thinking, which then pass them on to the church to serve as pastors.[11] The first problem is that it isolates the relationships among institutions to the "hand-offs," the transitions in the process of education. This lack of ongoing, meaningful relationships leads to a lack of trust among the partners. It is all too easy for the seminaries to complain that the churches do an ineffective job in formation, handing off candidates who are poorly grounded in the understandings and habits of the Christian faith. Similarly, it is all too easy for the churches to complain that the seminaries do an ineffective job in education, handing off clergy who are poorly prepared for their roles — and even causing some to lose their faith.

The second problem is that the model isolates the roles of the institutions, presuming that the formation of character belongs to the first leg of the race (congregations), critical inquiry belongs to the second leg (seminaries), and practicing skills of pastoral ministry belongs to the third leg (the congregations and other institutions the clergy go on to serve). This leads to a distortion among the institutions, presuming that the seminaries have only, or perhaps primarily, a role of providing critical inquiry rather than formation, and that congregations have no significant role in critical or constructive teaching and learning.

By contrast, we are suggesting that the task of learning is a life-long project for all Christians, including especially the clergy. There needs to be a rich interplay among congregations, seminaries, and other religious and social institutions throughout a person's formative education and ongoing learning. There is still the sense of a race, or at least a journey, with a goal toward which our learning and living is directed. But rather than a relay race, it is more like a pilgrimage that involves a variety of communal settings and institutions as partners on the journey toward God's kingdom. As congregations deepen their catechetical processes and ongoing patterns of cultivating Christian discipleship, they will discover creative and renewing ways to offer wisdom to, and receive insights from, seminaries. Likewise, as

11. These issues of theological education, and a proposal for the interactions among churches, seminaries, and settings of social engagement, are articulated more fully in L. Gregory Jones, "Beliefs, Desires, Practices, and the Ends of Theological Education," in *Practicing Theology*, ed. Miroslav Volf and Dorothy C. Bass (Grand Rapids: Eerdmans, 2002), pp. 185-205.

seminaries deepen their commitment to lifelong spiritual formation, they will discover creative and renewing ways to offer wisdom to, and receive insights from, congregations.

Further, both congregations and seminaries, at their best, will be involved with people's lives in the world and in settings and institutions of social engagement. Such involvement is critical for sustaining the reflection that helps shape laypersons' own capacities for their vocations as Christians, and for helping clergy and laity alike engage God's work in the world. Faithful living in the world draws Christians into contexts in which the distorting and sinful desires, practices, and structures of our world can be challenged by the light of the gospel. It also draws Christians into contexts, like the business leadership literature we discussed in Chapter 1, in which distortions within Christian congregations, seminaries, and other institutions can be illumined and addressed. Our witness in the world is informed by, and in turn informs, the normative practices of Christian catechesis. It will also be enriched by, and in turn enrich, the study of how desires, beliefs, and practices interrelate in an overall vision of God's inbreaking kingdom.

What, then, is the role of formal theological education? It is both more focused and more diffuse than many current assumptions. It is more focused in that theological education on this understanding has explicit partners in the task of equipping pastoral leaders. Hence, there is no longer a presumption that all of the learning needs to occur in the three or four years of a Master of Divinity program. Sometimes even strong and faithful seminaries struggle with competing expectations: they are to provide remedial catechesis, rigorous education, and practical training in a wide range of skills that are necessary, or at least useful, in a wide variety of ministry settings.

On the other hand, theological education has a more diffuse role, because it will develop ongoing connections with congregations, judicatories, pastors, and settings of social engagement. According to this model, seminaries will be institutions of lifelong learning, becoming involved with people at younger ages, with laity in other vocations, and with pastors throughout their ministries in a way that will be deeper and richer than the common contemporary model of "continuing education."

We are also suggesting that seminaries and divinity schools need a more complex self-understanding of their identity as "professional" schools. Insofar as they are preparing people for Christian pastoral ministry, they are necessarily involved in formation as well as education, in shaping character as well as conveying content and patterns of thinking, in nurturing holiness as well as equipping people with skills to be preachers, teachers, and leaders. Hence, their overall programs must nurture the intersecting capacities and gifts of calling, profession, and office for the pastoral vocation.

How, then, do we envision the importance of education for the clergy and the shape it should take? We believe there is much to be learned from Gregory the Great's analogy linking the vocations of clergy and physicians, and the notion that "the wounds of the mind are more hidden than the internal wounds of the body."

Gregory emphasizes the importance of excellent clergy. Because of the hiddenness of the wounds that they treat, clergy need to be well equipped with the skills of diagnosis. Of course, it is easier to pretend that one knows how to diagnose and treat these hidden wounds, precisely because they are hidden and the consequences of bad treatment are less immediately obvious than for physical wounds. Gregory notes that "although those who have no knowledge of the powers of drugs shrink from giving themselves out as physicians of the flesh, people who are utterly ignorant of spiritual precepts are often not afraid of professing themselves to be physicians of the heart. . . ."[12]

Gregory rightly believes that the stakes are high for the formation of clergy. Just as we want excellent physicians for the wounds of the body, so also we should want excellent clergy for the wounds of the mind and the soul. In a world that is rife with spiritual hucksters, how can we form faithful and effective "physicians of the heart"?

It is instructive to consider the formation of physicians in the United States. To be sure, the analogies are not perfect. Whereas those who are called to become clergy have already been involved in practices and friendships that have formed their character as disciples and are in continuity with their calling as clergy, physicians need have no prior engagement with the practice of medicine other than formal study in the sciences during undergraduate education.

Yet the ways in which physicians are formed in medical education

12. Gregory the Great, *Pastoral Care* 1.1, p. 21.

through a rich combination of classroom study, practice, and apprenticeship to master physicians offer significant analogies for theological education. There are certain basic patterns of feeling, thinking, and acting that need to be learned in and through the classroom, while there are other patterns and skills that can only be learned through apprenticeship.

Just as there are basic sciences that physicians must master, so there are basic understandings that are critical for the clergy to grasp. These include understandings of Scripture, key creeds and doctrines as well as the Lord's Prayer, the history of the church's faith and practices, and other crucial means of identifying the Triune God and distinguishing God from the myriad false gods — wealth, power, prestige, and so forth — that vie for our attention and allegiance. Those called to become clergy need to have made explicit that which in their discipleship has often remained implicit, and they need to be instructed more deeply and intentionally in the richness, complexity, and interrelations of the faith that they have heretofore engaged in more idiosyncratic, episodic, and often superficial ways. That is, there is a classical core content that is critically important for pastoral leaders to master.

It is equally important to have distorted understandings, images, and practices tested and revised. Theological education is a time for critical and constructive inquiry, for learning how to reason theologically and to discern faithful from idolatrous understandings of Christian faith and life. Further, there are basic tasks of preaching and worship that are intrinsically connected to interpreting Scripture and doctrine and hence depend on theological reasoning. Will Willimon has recently argued persuasively that in a time when many churches and pastors are focused on using techniques to make worship and preaching more interesting, the fundamental problem of poor preaching is theological — and its antidote is the excellent and imaginative theological interpretation of Scripture.[13]

Even so, the goal of classroom learning in theological education is not simply cognitive understanding, just as the goal of courses in basic sciences in medical school is not simply scientific research. Rather, the goal of theological education's classroom learning is to provide

13. William H. Willimon, *Proclamation and Theology* (Nashville: Abingdon, 2005).

content that can ultimately shape what Craig Dykstra has instructively described as a "pastoral imagination." We do not only want people who know Scripture, doctrine, history, and practices of Christian life. We want people who have been formed to learn how to attend to this knowledge with rich imaginative skill, to be able to reason practically at the intersections of this knowledge and the day-to-day tasks and relationships involved in pastoral ministry: celebrating the sacraments and leading worship, preaching biblically in imaginative ways, engaging with people from the youngest of children to the oldest of adults, celebrating the joys and griefs of life, and administering an organization of varying levels of complexity and size. Dykstra notes: "Life lived long enough and fully enough in the pastoral office gives rise to a distinctive imagination, a way of seeing in depth that is an indispensable gift to the church and its members."[14]

Such a pastoral imagination comes to life in preaching and teaching that bears faithful and powerful witness to God and God's reign. It is nourished by practices and friendships that sustain attentiveness to Scripture, to the fullness of the church's traditions, doctrines, and understandings, and to the extensive relationships with those people with whom the pastor is privileged to share ministry.

Dykstra notes that this pastoral imagination depends in a symbiotic way on an ecclesial imagination, the sort of "seeing in depth" that is cultivated among the whole Christian community. Stephen Fowl emphasizes the importance of this ecclesial imagination as it is developed in the Letter to the Philippians, especially chapter 2. We need pastors who can nurture congregations in imaginative reasoning through preaching and teaching, providing wise counsel and spiritual direction, and faithful and imaginative leadership and governance.

If those who are to become clergy are a part of such congregations, they will be well formed in their discipleship prior to their formal study, and during the time focused on learning in the classroom they will be continuing to engage in spiritual formation and other practices of Christian life. They will be cultivating habits that will be

14. Craig Dykstra, "Keys to Excellence: Pastoral Imagination and Holy Friendship." Available online at the Sustaining Pastoral Excellence (SPE) Web site, http://www.divinity.duke.edu/programs/spe/articles/200506/dykstra-p1.html. This material was first presented at an SPE forum, January 22, 2004.

sustained in their day-to-day lives in ministry.[15] Ideally, they will also begin to be exposed to the challenges and opportunities of pastoral leadership by becoming acquainted with particular skills as apprentices to pastors in congregations, hospitals, prisons, or other settings.

Here again the medical school analogy is instructive: if the aim is to form physicians rather than scientists, there are understandings, gifts, and skills that can only be learned through practice and apprenticeship to wise physicians. This is done both through rounds in the hospital and through residencies. Unfortunately, because of the "relay race" model, we have been insufficiently attentive to the need for those who are learning to become pastoral leaders to be engaged in practice and apprenticeship to wise clergy. Too often graduates of seminary are simply sent out into ministry as if they were already fully formed and ready for their vocation.

Surgeon Atul Gawande describes the awkwardness, and the difficulty, of first trying to learn how to translate what he had learned in the books to the practice of surgery itself. Gawande writes: "In surgery, as in anything else, skill and confidence are learned through experience — haltingly and humiliatingly. Like the tennis player and the oboist and the guy who fixes hard drives, we need practice to get good at what we do. There is one difference in medicine, though: it is people we practice upon."[16] So also with pastors.

Gawande notes studies that have shown that, as with the "practiced" commitment of excellence, more important to learning a skill than native talent are the discipline and attention to detail involved in frequent practice itself. Moreover, there will be long stretches of frustration and stagnation that suddenly give way to breakthroughs in the learning. Gawande observes: "Practice is funny that way. For days and days, you make out only the fragments of what to do. And then one day you've got the thing whole. Conscious learning becomes unconscious knowledge, and you cannot say precisely how."[17] Similarly, the cultivation of a pastoral imagination requires attentive-

15. See the descriptions in many of Eugene Peterson's writings, especially *Working the Angles: The Shape of Pastoral Integrity* (Grand Rapids: Eerdmans, 1987). He emphasizes there the three essential acts of ministry involved in paying attention to God: prayer, Scripture, and spiritual direction.

16. Atul Gawande, *Complications* (New York: Henry Holt, 2002), p. 18.

17. Gawande, *Complications*, p. 21.

ness to frequent practice and to learning the ways in which wise clergy embody the subtle, even "unconscious" knowledge that has become a part of the very way in which they see God, the world, themselves, and others.

Such wise clergy can see possibilities that are not currently there, and they also see what Dykstra calls the "more" in what is already there. They have nurtured these gifts over time, and they always continue to learn. Gawande notes that for surgeons the process of learning extends throughout a lifetime.[18] Should we imagine that it would take any less time, energy, or focus for clergy, given that we are dealing with the care of souls?

Formal theological education is an essential part of the process of learning to become clergy. Yet we need to reimagine the shape of that education, both in its connections to congregations and settings of social engagement on the one hand and in its attention to the importance of apprenticeship to mentors and learning skills of practice on the other. The goal of cultivating a pastoral imagination through distinctive, lifelong learning is to equip people for leadership that will create spirals of faithfulness among those with whom they are in ministry. Dykstra describes it well: "In the wake of mutual encouragement, true excellence in ministry — communal to its marrow, never individual — both arises and reproduces itself. Ministry like this has about it a kind of beauty and allure that is almost irresistible. And so it replicates itself by drawing more and more people into it, forming and shaping their lives and imaginations, and launching them into new ministry in turn. Such ministry has about it a freshness, an improvisatory character, a liveliness that is itself infectious. And thus an imagination that is at its heart a 'seeing in depth' turns out to be an imagination full of creativity — an imagination that sees what is 'not yet' and begins to create it."[19]

We have suggested that the symbiotic relationship between an ecclesial imagination and a pastoral imagination, learned and lived in partnership with formal theological education and other religious in-

18. He writes: "Surgical training is the recapitulation of this process — the floundering followed by fragments, followed by knowledge and occasionally a moment of elegance — over and over again, for ever harder tasks with ever greater risks." See Gawande, *Complications*, p. 22.

19. Dykstra, "Keys to Excellence."

stitutions and settings of social engagement, invites an improvisational approach to leadership and governance that is both faithful and creative. What would such an approach entail?

Practice: The Art of Improvisational Leadership

In a recent book about Christian ethics, Samuel Wells develops the idea of "improvisation" as a key theme for Christian life. His account, a description of how the church might envision the Christian life, has significant implications for pastoral leadership. He develops in similar ways Dykstra's emphasis on the imagination, and he illumines why it is that in times of institutional change attention to the formation of character is so critical.

Underlying Wells's account is his conviction that the time of the church, the time in which Christians live, is the fourth act in a five-act drama. The first three acts are creation, Israel, and Jesus. The fifth act is the eschaton, the time when God will bring the creation to its completion. Because of the power of the third act and the promise of the fifth, the fourth act is a time of freedom — a time, Wells says, when Christians "are not called to be effective or successful, but to be faithful."[20] It does not all depend on us, because the drama is the work of God. The fourth act is a time of active receptivity, in which we are called and encouraged to respond to God's work through improvisational creativity.

The key, according to Wells, lies in the cultivation of habits and dispositions through rehearsal. Most of our time, in improvisational theater or in life, is spent in rehearsal — in training. Wells writes: "This ability 'to see simultaneously what is and what might yet be' is the creative force of training in how to live well — otherwise known as moral formation. The pain and care of schooling in a tradition is about learning to see the ambiguity of the world truthfully, yet maintaining hope. The practice of the moral life, meanwhile, is not so much about being creative or clever as it is about taking the right things for granted."[21]

20. Samuel Wells, *Improvisation* (Grand Rapids: Brazos, 2004), p. 55.
21. Wells, *Improvisation*, p. 76.

We learn to take the right things for granted through discipleship, the cultivation of an ecclesial imagination that enables us to develop the eyes to see and ears to hear God and God's work in the world. Faithful discipleship prepares us to be attentive. Again, Wells is instructive: "There is no place for the complacency that says all is well or the despair that says all is lost. There is instead a balance between the concentrated effort of our drawing near to God and the surprising grace of his drawing near to us. In this argument I am suggesting that the categories of effort and habit may find theological partners in the categories of discipleship and grace. If Christians have learned to take the right things for granted (discipleship) they will more readily experience God's ways with them and the world (grace)."[22]

Wells's account wonderfully displays why the formation of character, and especially the more intensive formation for pastoral leadership, is so critical for the holiness of heart and life necessary for preaching and teaching, celebrating the sacraments, and offering wise counsel. Even more, it shows the importance of that character for wise and faithful leadership in shaping communities and leading institutions, especially in times of change.

Too often, and particularly in recent decades, Christians in America have taken the wrong things for granted: the existence of religious institutions, for example. We have presumed that their permanence is a given and that our key task is to manage them as the regrettably necessary structures for the practices and friendships that really give life to Christian community. The unfortunate result is that many of them have lost their Christian vitality, their Christian focus and direction. This is true of congregations as well as judicatories, of seminaries and colleges as well as health care institutions — indeed, whole networks of religious institutions whose ecology has been crucial to shaping Christian life and imagination.

Part of the problem, as we have already suggested, is that we have too often accepted the romantic view that real vitality is to be found in practices and friendships, and institutions are at best necessary evils. The theological version of this view is to imagine that Jesus and a ragtag bunch of radical disciples had a wonderful community that, over time after Jesus' death and resurrection, hardened into dreaded insti-

---

22. Wells, *Improvisation*, pp. 77-78.

tutions — what is sometimes in the literature called, usually pejoratively, "early Catholicism." We carry with us a mistaken myth that institutions are at best the necessary chaff that we must winnow in order to find the pure wheat of the gospel. But that is not faithful to Scripture (it ignores Israel and its institutions, among other things), and it is not faithful to the empirical realities of our life together. We need to reclaim an understanding of what is involved in the creation and renovation, sustenance and extension of institutions that do indeed need criticism from time to time. But the romantic notion that we are somehow going to find a purer community apart from the reality of institutions is fallacious.

Another part of the problem is simple inattention, our failure to think theologically and imaginatively about leading religious institutions. Wells's analysis helps us see how we might address an improvisational challenge that God is presenting to us in the present and for the future: the cultivation and formation of pastoral leaders who can create, renovate, sustain, and extend our religious institutions.

We cannot address this challenge with anything approximating the full treatment it needs and deserves. However, we do want to describe three characteristic roles of pastoral leaders that are crucial for the faithful and effective governance of religious institutions: interpreters, visionaries, and reconcilers. The core qualities of each of the three are basic to all Christian discipleship. Even so, it is important to discover and cultivate leaders who are particularly gifted in these capacities and who can in turn equip others as fellow interpreters, visionaries, and reconcilers.

What might leadership marked by these capacities look like? Greg and his wife encountered a striking portrait of such ministry on a poignant visit to a pair of remarkable congregations in South Africa.

As they traveled to the churches in the summer of 2000, their hearts were heavy from seeing the legacy of pain and suffering of apartheid South Africa. They had encountered significant brokenness across the country, and much despair about the future. But when they arrived at these settings of ministry, their hearts began to lift. They discovered two Methodist congregations, one predominantly white, the other black, that were committed to a ministry of reconciliation. The two congregations had begun an explicit, costly, life-giving partnership with each other. The predominantly white congregation was in an upper-middle-class community north of Johannesburg, while the black congregation was a few miles away in one of many desperately poor townships.

Despite their profound differences, these congregations were committed to one another as Christians. Greg described the experience for our colloquium: "During the time we spent there, we learned about vital practices of a deeply shared life, engaged in conversations with whites and blacks whose lives had been transformed, and witnessed new ministries of outreach that stirred our imaginations. These congregations were ambitious for the gospel."

What made this partnership a setting for such excellent ministry? First, the two pastors were people of deep learning, passionate Christian commitment, and imaginative graciousness. They were wise interpreters: each of them read widely, and they were asking important and provocative questions. They were also visionaries, encouraging each other, and their laity, to think honestly about their life together and to imagine new ways of faithful discipleship. And they were reconcilers, working actively to overcome past injustices in very tangible ways.

These capacities were evident as they talked about their vision for the future. Everything they described had a reference point theologically and was focused on a ministry of reconciliation. Indeed, the predominantly white congregation's new sanctuary had been designed with a clear theological focus: a baptismal font in the sanctuary with regularly flowing water, spaces for gathering and conversation, and — perhaps most powerfully — a large "embracing" cross outside the sanctuary with these words inscribed at its foot:

> This cross is shaped to express God's loving embrace of the world in the death of Jesus. The left arm is raised higher and extends further than the right arm because it is the extension of the heart, reminding us that Jesus' heart was given in obedience to the Father in his work of boundless loving. The left arm is also the arm of the outcast, reminding us that Jesus came to raise the lowly and poor. The shortened right arm symbolises the powerful who are humbled and brought low, as prophesied by Mary in Luke 1:51-53.
>
> In our land, for so long defined and wounded by exclusion and separation, the Embracing Cross of Christ is a sign of hope and

healing. May God strengthen us to become a people of welcome and healing embrace! 1st Sunday of Advent, 1999[23]

Interpreters

The words inscribed at the foot of that cross were informed by the Christian experience of pastors and laity who were equally attentive to the past and to the signs of the times. Interpreters are a community's custodians of both memory and hope, people who help set the challenges and opportunities of the present within the much larger context of what God has done in the past and where God is leading in the future. There may be a number of interpreters within a community, not all of them primary leaders, but it is critically important that those entrusted with leadership be particularly gifted in this capacity.

The task of interpretation was a shared ministry in the two South African congregations. The two churches conducted "pilgrimages of pain and hope" in each other's communities. Laypeople from each church would invite members of the other church to come and stay with them in their homes. Obviously, this entailed significant discomfort for both sides as each community discovered how the other lived. But such reciprocal hospitality enabled the two communities to learn to listen to each other's history and experience and to understand one another at a deeper level. Throughout their ministries, they continued to pay attention to the importance of what we will later describe as "counterweighting," of finding the means to keep their relationships and activities in some measure of just equilibrium as they undertook transformative ministry.

One key activity of the interpreter is to nurture continuity with tradition. Just as in theater and in music, improvisation in leadership is effective only when its practitioners are deeply attentive to what has gone on before them. That includes not only the immediate past but, importantly, the more distant past as well. To be sure, it is tempting to try to ignore the past, because it can burden and haunt the present. But the past can also offer signs of faithfulness and new life. In nurtur-

23. L. Gregory Jones, "A Ministry of Reconciliation" (Colloquium on Excellence in Ministry, Duke Divinity School, Durham, NC, May 17-18, 2001), p. 1.

ing continuity with the past, tradition must be distinguished from what Jaroslav Pelikan calls "traditionalism": "Traditionalism is the dead faith of the living," he says; "tradition is the living faith of the dead."[24]

Too many leaders assume that they arrive at a new position or a new institution with a blank slate, a freedom to begin with their own vision and big ideas irrespective of the past. Continuity with tradition calls us to recognize that the particular character of an institution, how it thinks and lives, has been shaped by generations who have gone before. This happens in ways that are sometimes explicit and sometimes implicit; sometimes life-giving and sometimes corrupt and ideologically distorted. Churches, seminaries, and universities often tell the story of their past in romanticized ways. But to nurture continuity with tradition is to recognize that our current identity, our current manner of thinking and living, has been shaped for both good and ill by the complexity of the past. Ken Carder's experience in Mississippi, which we looked at in an earlier chapter, is a powerful example of this recognition, but even in the most ordinary circumstances, the narratives of the past, richly shared, can enliven the present and future.

Interpreters who cultivate continuity with tradition display a trust that our predecessors have also sought to be faithful, amidst the challenges and sins that mark all of our lives. Moreover, and more determinatively, they display a trust in the power of God's Holy Spirit to continue to work in the world and people's lives to bring life out of death, and to preserve faithfulness even amidst brokenness and sin. In this regard, they seek to embody repentance and to lead others to do so as well. These leaders understand that we need to repent and be forgiven of our failures of the past even as we heed God's call to live into the future.

One of the great biblical texts demonstrating the sinful rejection of the call to live into the future is the story of the spies in Numbers 13 and 14. In this story, twelve spies are sent to scout out the promised land. They come back with a majority and a minority report. The majority of ten says, in effect, "We can't go forward. It's a land flowing with milk and honey, but there are giants up ahead. There are too many

24. Jaroslav Pelikan, *The Vindication of Tradition* (New Haven: Yale University Press, 1984), p. 65.

obstacles." Only two of the twelve, Joshua and Caleb, say, in effect, "We have to go forward. God is calling us there, and if God is calling us, we can trust God for the future." The fearful Israelites side with the majority and respond, in effect, "Let's go back to Egypt." Egypt represented slavery, oppression, and suffering — but it was familiar.

Every local church we've ever known has had a "Back to Egypt" committee in it. Indeed, all of us have a "Back to Egypt" part of our souls. But wise pastoral leadership is imaginative and improvisational, looking creatively toward the future and trusting that the God we worship is the God not only of yesterday and today but also of tomorrow.

Thinking creatively for the future, a key task for interpreters, means exploring how institutions need to grow, adapt, and change in order to be faithful. It also includes discernment about what new institutions need to be created. Too often we take congregations and other institutions for granted, forgetting the risks that our forebears took in faithfulness and creativity as they sought to embody the strongest witness to God they could envision.

Visionaries

As interpreters preserve an institution's memory and hope, it is critically important that they take "the long view." This has both personal and institutional dimensions. Visionary leaders take the long view personally, learning how to be silent rather than speaking too quickly. Leaders are often tempted to speak hastily, saying what seems good at the moment but compromising the institution over the long term. Too often leaders fail to interpret what is going on in a larger context, acting only for short-term interests and wreaking havoc when patience might have permitted greater faithfulness and stability. Visionary leaders recognize that good things must be nurtured over time: sometimes only the seed of an idea is going to be planted by the leader, while the nurturing and reaping will be done by the leader's successors.

Further, visionaries will attend to redemptive silence as well as speech, learning to discern when it seems "good to the Holy Spirit and to us" (Acts 15:28, the conclusion of the Council of Jerusalem). There is no "me" in that description. It is not about the vision of one person; rather, it involves the discernment and interpretation of the whole community. Taking the long view focuses on a sense of "ripeness" for movement among the whole institution. It does not mean waiting forever. It does not mean necessarily avoiding hard decisions and decisive actions, letting the chips fall where they may. What it does mean is that when hard decisions and decisive actions are undertaken, visionary leaders are careful to count the cost and weigh the implications.

Visionaries also take the long view institutionally, remembering that we are only the fourth act of a five-act drama, to return to Wells's metaphor, and that institutions endure over time. There is freedom in knowing that the fifth act is God's. But there is also responsibility, for while the fifth act could come at any time, we must care for institutions with a view to the prospect that they will last for decades and, potentially, centuries. Hence, we should be patient — not passive but patient, a virtue that points to the quality of our attention and our care. Patience reminds us that our life is a response to the gift of God's grace, and that we are called to attend to God rather than just forcing our own will on things — whether institutions, other persons, or our own lives.

Leaders of institutions need to be able to see what is as well as what might be. How is that gift of vision cultivated among pastoral leaders? The secular literature on leadership often describes the importance of "casting a vision," "articulating a vision," and then mobilizing people around that vision. Such emphases are important in moving people beyond mere management to envisioning what might be possible. But for Christians, this is not a task exclusive to the leader (as also, we would suggest, it ought not be even in secular institutions). Rather, visionary leaders involve the whole community in the Christian practice of discernment, helping them imagine possibilities and then take faithful risks that they might otherwise be unwilling to take.

We are the beneficiaries of visionary leaders who have been willing to think big in creating institutions that serve important human needs. These are leaders who have founded colleges and universities, established hospitals and children's homes, conceived cathedrals and symphonies. Yet in contemporary America, big dreams and ambitious goals seem now to have become the property of Hollywood moguls, medical researchers, and technology entrepreneurs.

Too many churches and institutions seem to be trapped in a narrative of decline. Meetings tend to be more about financial cutbacks, discouragement over membership losses, and diminished influence. When "big" ideas are proposed in mainline denominations, they are too often merely quick-fix solutions to technical problems, imposed on unsuspecting and hence uninspired communities and institutions.

To be sure, not all big dreams involve large scale and scope. Big thinking often occurs in small situations, as God repeatedly displays in Scripture. A big commitment to beauty can be evidenced in something exquisitely simple. Further, it requires thinking big to imagine even the smallest acts of reconciliation within a community that has been estranged, and it takes extraordinary trust and passion to discover new life in small situations that have been left for dead. Heidi Neumark's ministry in the South Bronx, for example, was marked by thinking big in unpredictable but faithful ways.

Visionary Christian leaders focus not on their own personal vision or ambition but rather on the welfare of the organization. As we described in Chapter 1, Jim Collins discovered that this characterized the highest level of gifted business leaders in "good to great" institutions. This suggests that we need pastoral leaders who are not preoccupied with status or with the goal of getting particular positions. Such people covet positions for the wrong reasons — the salary, or power, or recognition, or just for being the next step on the ladder of success. The church calls people into positions of leadership because gifts are discerned, not because power is coveted. Granted, there are multiple ways that people can display false humility and play games with that sort of activity. But we long for leaders who are focused, not on themselves, but on helping institutions to embody a faithful witness to God.

In order effectively to facilitate such a witness, visionary leaders need to be able to exercise authority wisely for the sake of the whole community or institution. This requires a convergence of being *in* authority and being *an* authority. There is a certain credibility, of power and influence, that comes from office — from being in authority. But in wise leaders, that authority converges with the credibility of character, of being an authority. Such leaders are not afraid of exercising that authority and that power for the sake of the institution. Perhaps the most powerful contemporary example of such convergence in a visionary leader is that of Desmond Tutu in South Africa. He held an office as the Anglican Archbishop of Cape Town, and that office converged with a powerful moral and theological vision that eventually exceeded his office.

Integral to the wise use of authority is a willingness to admit mistakes and learn from failure. This is difficult because, in a culture of "experts," people fear that if we acknowledge mistakes, we will be perceived as weak leaders. So there is a temptation to cover them up, to gloss them over, to put them in the passive voice. Exodus 32 and 33 reveal this perennial problem in the story of the golden calf. When Aaron is confronted by Moses about the calf, he responds that he threw the people's gold into the fire, "and out came this calf!" (Exod. 32:24). A magical event — no one did it; it just happened. The temptation of any leader is to evade responsibility through the passive voice — mistakes were made, but nobody made them. And yet, when we can genuinely acknowledge failure, and the vulnerability that goes with it, then we have the capacity to learn from that failure in a way that empowers both our leadership and the institution. We observed a bishop of a denomination confess administrative mistakes and failure in front of the diocese, asking forgiveness from the gathering, and we saw the transforming difference it made. It actually enabled more effective and faithful leadership, because he was no longer seen as someone exercising externalized authority and power but as someone with whom they were in ministry together.

Visionary leaders have a capacity for the prophetic use of power in both cursing and blessing. We most easily associate prophetic use of power with critique: challenging incompetence, bearing witness against injustice, criticizing loveless indifference as well as bureaucratic structures that sap the energy from people and systems, calling for the kind of confident leadership that says, "This ought not be so."

Yet prophetic power is not only about cursing; it is also about blessing. The story of Balaam's donkey in Numbers 22–24 is important for discovering visionary leadership, especially the prophetic use of power, as an offering of blessing. Balaam can exercise prophecy only when he discovers that he is no smarter than a donkey. But the prophecy that God then puts into his mouth is a command to bless. Balaam says, "How fair are your tents, O Jacob, your encampments, O Israel!" (Numbers 24:5). It is easier to be a prophet who just baldly speaks the truth in critical and denunciatory ways. Even so, wise, visionary leadership of institutions calls both for prophetic critique and prophetic blessing.

Prophetic power calls for ongoing discernment about the needs of the community, its members, and the surrounding culture. Professor Stephen Long writes: "Prophetic preaching is not heroic. . . . The prophetic preacher stands under the community of faith; he or she is not set over and against it. To be prophetic is not in opposition to being pastoral. Prophetic preaching is the most pastoral of activities."[25] What is true of preaching is also true of the fullness of the pastoral life. Indeed, in situations of significant brokenness, fragmentation, and division, the most visionary, prophetic ministries may be the ones that are marked by care, civility, and interpretive charity extended towards others' speech and actions.

Interpreters discern carefully the ways of God in leading us from the past to the future; visionaries see their communities and institutions in relation to the abundance of God's grace and the *telos* of God's kingdom, and are willing to exercise authority and power wisely in service of that vision. Yet we also need to cultivate reconcilers, leaders who draw people together, sustain communities, and minimize the sense in which anyone feels marginalized.

Reconcilers

Paul describes in 2 Corinthians 5:16-19 the crucial task of reconciliation as an activity for all Christians, as we bear witness to the "new creation" discovered in Christ. Christians are called to a ministry of reconciliation, and indeed Paul notes that God has entrusted "the message of reconciliation to us." Yet discerning how to embody that message is not easy; we need leaders who are gifted at the gestures, strategies, and words that make reconciliation real in people's lives, in institutions, and in the wider world.

One key activity of reconcilers is "counterweighting." This is an image that comes from the Irish poet Seamus Heaney, who learned it from Simone Weil. Heaney describes it as the idea of "balancing out the forces, of redress — tilting the scales of reality towards some tran-

25. D. Stephen Long, "Prophetic Preaching," in *Concise Encyclopedia of Preaching,* ed. William H. Willimon and Richard Lischer (Louisville: Westminster John Knox, 1995), p. 388.

scendent equilibrium."[26] The activity of counterweighting involves trying to avoid any sense of permanent "losers." In any institution, in any gathered community over time, different interest groups and divisions will develop. Ideally, they become crosscutting rather than entrenched, but part of a reconciler's task is to use counterweighting to keep a sense of balance. This does not mean becoming like the church of Laodicea in Revelation 3, to whom the Lord says, "Because you are lukewarm, and neither cold nor hot, I am about to spit you out of my mouth" (v. 16). Counterweighting is not a lukewarm moderation that has nothing to offer but rather a dynamic "centering" that tilts the scales back and forth to maintain a balance over time.

This tilting has a crucial role to play in the task of interpretive leadership as well. At times, the counterweighting calls us to attend more to preserving tradition, because too much change can result in chaos. At other times, it calls us to take greater risks, because too much focus on tradition can become stifling. This important activity of leadership is different from the popular image of "leading change," which can too often result in imbalance and chaos. By contrast, attention to "counterweighting" focuses on consistently holding things in balance, attending to polarities that can otherwise stifle institutional vitality and even result in destructive conflicts and a sense of permanent marginalization or loss.[27]

Another task of reconciling leaders is what Sam Wells calls "overaccepting," a term borrowed from improvisational theater.[28] This is a practice central to the biblical story, and especially the ministry of Jesus. It builds on the interpretive tasks of nurturing the continuity of

26. See Seamus Heaney, *The Redress of Poetry* (New York: Farrar, Straus & Giroux, 1996), p. 3. Heaney draws from Simone Weil, *Gravity and Grace*, trans. Emma Crawford and Mario von der Ruhr (1947; London: Routledge, 2002). We are grateful to United Methodist Bishop Timothy Whitaker for pointing us to the significance of this image for pastoral leadership.

27. An alternative image to "leading change" is "polarity management," which is very close to what we are calling counterweighting. We are hesitant to employ the term "management" here, as we see the task of attending to polarities as a central work of leadership. Even so, this movement of "polarity management" usefully challenges the presumption that change is always to be desired. See Barry Johnson, *Polarity Management* (Amherst, Mass.: HRD Press, 1992). We are grateful to John Wimmer for directing us to this insightful account.

28. See Wells, *Improvisation*, chapter 9, especially pp. 131ff.

tradition and thinking creatively for the future. What does overaccepting involve? When a person in improvisational theater receives an "offer" — a communication, verbal or nonverbal, from another actor that invites a response — there are two obvious options. The person can "accept" the offer, that is, respond in a way that carries forward its premise, and the story goes on. Or the person can "block" the offer — undermine or negate it. The difficulty with blocking is that there is no way to go forward.

So there is a third alternative, to "overaccept." Overaccepting is an activity of accepting an offer with a view to a larger story, moving it forward by reconceiving it in a new and redemptive way. Wells argues that this is how God's reign functions: "God does not block his creation: he does not toss away his original material. Since Noah, he has refused to destroy what he has made. But neither does he accept creation on its own terms. Instead, he overaccepts his creation. One can see the whole sweep of the scriptural narrative as a long story of overaccepting."[29] Jesus overaccepts the Pharisees when he refuses their traditionalist traps, offering a new way of conceiving issues that both nurtures continuity with tradition and cultivates creativity for the future.

Reconciling leaders are called to overaccept by taking the concerns and offers of others, whether the world or particular people or institutions, and finding ways to accept them by reconceiving them in the light of God's reign. This is done with particular people by finding ways to draw them into the larger vision, seeing possibilities in them that they may not be able to see in themselves, and offering them signs of grace and love. With institutions, overaccepting involves discovering ways to enable change by reconceiving potentially divisive issues in the context of God's work in the world. For example, as we described in Chapter 1, Heidi Neumark overaccepted the children who were baptized and "of course" were given a new identity; and she overaccepted the potential closing of the church by reconceiving the church's ministry in terms of the death and resurrection of Christ.

Reconciling leaders are proficient in the activity of "reincorporating the lost," another term Wells deploys from improvisational theater. This task affirms the value and indeed necessity of continually looking back and retrieving aspects of the story that have been left out

29. Wells, *Improvisation*, p. 134.

or lost. It entails remembering the sins of the past as well as the lives of the saints. It also entails paying close attention to those who have been, and still are, marginalized as well as those who are at the center of power. Wells writes: "[T]he church needs to maintain a lively memory, in which it recalls tales of the good and the bad, and especially of those who have not written their own history — the losers. The greatest improvisers, such as [St.] Laurence, did nothing more than reincorporate discarded elements of the story. To do this, one has to be part of a community that knows and lives the story."[30]

This task of reincorporating the lost requires ongoing discernment and counterweighting. In cultures of power, it means carefully attending to those who are powerless. But it also means guarding against so narrow a focus on those who are on the margins that we instead marginalize those who are in positions of influence. We can never rest content with a notion of permanent insiders and outsiders.

Reincorporation of the lost is a part of Christian excellence that is patterned in the life, death, and resurrection of Jesus Christ. Our capacity for such reincorporation, whether in our own lives, in institutions, or in the larger world, is a sign that we recognize that authentic excellence involves a truthfulness of memory and of life. Such truthful remembering, grounded in a forgiveness that acknowledges and redeems the past, also calls us to truthful attention to that which is lost in our own midst. It is focused on a ministry of reconciliation.

*   *   *

Wise pastoral leadership calls us to lead communities and institutions as interpreters, visionaries, and reconcilers. It is a challenging vocation, and we will not be equally gifted in all of these capacities, even as we seek to develop them in their interrelations. Even so, this call points us toward the high bar, and the high stakes, of resurrecting excellence in ministry. The more faithfully we cultivate the capacities to be interpreters, visionaries, and reconcilers, the more faithfully we will embody the ambition for the gospel to which we are called by the Triune God.

To be sure, this call can seem daunting — even overwhelming. We

30. Wells, *Improvisation*, p. 151.

understand that, and sympathize — but we do not intend for it to be perceived as a burden. Quite the contrary. We would suggest that the overwhelming itself can be experienced as a blessing, a part of the life, patterned in Christ, that is "a still more excellent way." To help frame this perspective, we offer three brief observations.

First, our calling to serve as pastoral leaders is always a gift before it is a task, a response to God's grace. We are only the fourth act in the drama, not the fifth. So while the stakes are high, there is room for improvisation and creativity, and even room for failure. We are also reminded that there are important rhythms of rest and play as well as work, and that practices of Sabbath-keeping and renewal are integral parts of what it means to pattern our lives in the grace and new life of Christ's resurrection.

Second, the overwhelming to which we are called is not debilitating but empowering. We are called to be overwhelmed by the abundance of God's grace, love, mercy, generosity, and joy. David Ford suggests that living into "the overwhelming" of God's grace is the most profound learning we can discover, and the only real route to goodness and virtue. He writes: "The strange truth is, therefore, that there is no direct way to goodness. We do not construct a good life by deciding to obey certain teachings, to follow our conscience, to stick to certain principles, to do our duty, to imitate good examples, or to develop virtues and good habits. There is something more fundamental than that sort of action. It is more like the 'active passivity' of letting ourselves be embraced, or letting ourselves be fed the food and drink that can energize us for virtue. I have been calling it 'being overwhelmed.' The way to goodness is through being immersed in that multiple 'how much more . . .' of Romans 5. It leads straight to the secret of transformed living in Romans 6. . . ."[31]

Third, a central means by which we pattern our lives in Christ, and discover the overwhelming grace of being embraced by God, is by attending to the treasures of the gospel that sustain us over time. These treasures, often overlooked as we reflect on excellence in Christian life and ministry, are intrinsically important to our life with God. It is to an account of these treasures of excellent ministry that we now turn.

---

31. David Ford, *The Shape of Living* (Grand Rapids: Baker, 1997), p. 89.

$\widehat{6}$ *The Treasures of*
       Excellent Ministry

"For where your treasure is, there your heart will be also." Packed in one short verse, Luke 12:34, is wisdom that enlivens nearly all our conversations about excellent ministry. Holy friendships are among our most precious estate, but there are other resources as well that reveal the heart's desire and capacity for resurrecting excellence in Christian ministry. How we cultivate the formative, imaginative, institutional, and economic resources of shared ministry reflects our yearnings — and sometimes our disregard — for resurrecting excellence. A heart for resurrecting excellence will create, commend, and preserve these precious resources so that ministry is enlivened and sustained over time.

We refer to these resources as treasures for three important and closely related reasons. First, they are shared resources, and not simply individual possessions. A closer look at Luke's translation of Jesus' statement reveals that Luke uses the plural "your" with both heart and treasure. The treasures we describe are not simply personal belongings to claim or cast off. They are mutual resources that come to us as gifts bearing substance, wisdom, and tradition. They have been infused with the Holy Spirit, tested over time, and sustained precisely because they are shared and not privately held. Such mutuality has shaping power for the community: attentiveness to *our* treasures can help us imagine our hearts joined together in ministry.

We also refer to these resources as treasures because they are intrinsically valuable to our identity and purpose. Treasures convey the character of a community even as they help it articulate where it is going and how it will get there. In other words, treasures are not merely functional resources, with a limited shelf life. Some resources serve to help us through the next liturgical season or stewardship campaign. They are valuable but short-lived. Our treasures help us articulate who we are and who we hope to become.

Finally, we want to be clear that while treasures in Christianity as we experience it in contemporary America are sometimes well hidden, they are not scarce. We believe that formative, imaginative, institutional, and economic treasures are abundant. We have seen these treasures uncovered and shared in affluent suburban congregations as well as churches in impoverished neighborhoods and rural communities. Vital treasures are found in large judicatories, institutions, and agencies as well as in smaller gatherings of clergy, neighborhood activists, and lay ministry teams. Treasures are abundant. What we often lack is a coherent, enlivened vision of how to attend to these treasures so they may become an aid — and not an obstruction — on the journey to the "everlasting holy places." As we discover the treasures at God's banquet table, we must reimagine how we offer and receive these good treasures so they may become as bread and wine for our life together.

Discovering and cultivating God's treasures is neither predictable nor instinctive. We need ways of living that keep us attentive to God, "who by the power at work within us is able to accomplish abundantly far more than all we can ask or imagine" (Eph. 3:20). Such attentiveness is particularly important when the treasures among us have become hidden, stale, or spoiled. Ministries of resurrecting excellence are grounded in an attentiveness that arises from Christian practices.[1]

The formative and imaginative treasures of our faith — Scripture, theology, hymns, prayers, literature, arts, and community — are engaged through practices such as reading, study, singing, prayer, wise governance, hospitality, and forgiveness. Just as all treasures are shared, all Christian practices are communal. The treasure of biblical wisdom becomes more obvious and radiant as faithful people read and study together. Even solitary reading and study bring us into relation-

1. We are grateful to Stephanie Paulsell for her expression of the relationship between treasures and practices that follows.

ship with all who have ever read and studied and all who ever will. The institutional treasures connected to our faith — congregations, schools, foundations, hospitals, publishing houses, daycare centers, homeless shelters — require the practice of wise governance. Even the economic treasures — salaries, grants, tithes, financial subsidies — are most fully revealed when rooted in practices of prayer, discernment, and testimony. Faithful people who pattern their lives by these practices, and who invite others to do the same, create a culture of resurrecting excellence.

This culture is a reflection of Jesus' own life. The Gospels describe Jesus as pointing to and uncovering the treasures of a community even when the distractions and demands of others were swirling around him, and perhaps even churning within him. The treasures his disciples enjoyed were rooted in Jesus' habits and commendation of Sabbath, prayer, hospitality, and testimony. A woman's life was saved and the treasure of living more abundantly together revealed when Jesus offered forgiveness and conveyed to others the beauty of such a practice.

The practices by which we engage the treasures of our faith cultivate in us the attention to God, one another, and the world that allows ministries of resurrecting excellence to flourish. Whether we are establishing wise habits of administration and governance that enable us to discover and use the treasures among us, or reading Scripture deeply enough for it to become written on our minds and hearts, we are opening the places in our lives where God can reach us, where we can reach out to the world, and where the treasures of resurrecting excellence can flourish.

It is essential to identify the treasures necessary to sustain Christian ministry and discern the vocations to ordained ministry within the church. These treasures help us test and grow in our judgments about a faithful life. But we also need to consider the complicated and important issue of how we engage these resources. Who has access to them, and who does not? Will we allow the cultural patterns and practices around us to set our terms and modes of engagement, or will we as communities of faith be intentional in the way we order our lives to engage them? Understanding the latter question involves examining the forces of the larger culture that inhibit and enliven excellence.

We begin with an exploration of the formative and imaginative treasures that reside among us: Scripture and theology, hymns and prayers, poetry and literature, and a variety of arts. We then turn to institutional treasures — healthy institutions and organizations that should be sustained, fragile ones in need of healing, fading ones perhaps in need of a good death, and emerging ones awaiting a midwife. Finally, we explore some of the economic treasures of ministry: pastoral compensation, funding for theological education, and financial resources among churches and the larger culture. These categories are neither exhaustive nor rigidly defined. Indeed, the banquet table holding God's treasures stretches out in all directions, certainly beyond where we currently imagine.

Formative and Imaginative Treasures

Scripture and Theology

If God is our primary referent for excellence, then our encounter with God's word is one of our greatest treasures.[2] We human readers are like the stars in the firmament, St. Augustine speculated, clinging to the strange, old words of Scripture with both our hands, trying to catch a glimpse of God through its veil. To be human, for Augustine, is to be a reader. Augustine imagined that the angels, on the other side of the veil, read as well — not words, but the very face of God. Their reading, unlike ours, is perpetual, "and what they read never passes away."[3] The spoken and written word, for Augustine, is temporal and fleeting as well as eternal and inbreaking. At the intersection of the words and the Word, we encounter our treasure. Well attended, this treasure is our primary map. Ignored, it is powerless to direct our journey.

In Pulpit & Pew's recent survey of Christian clergy in the United States, more than half of the respondents indicated that one of their primary problems in today's world is difficulty in reaching people

2. Again, Stephanie Paulsell urged us to consider this perspective in her paper "Excellence in Ministry and the Practice of Reading" (Colloquium on Excellence in Ministry, Duke Divinity School, Durham, N.C., May 16-17, 2002).

3. Augustine, *Confessions*, trans. Henry Chadwick (New York: Oxford University Press, 1991), 13.18.22, p. 285; 13.15.18, p. 283.

with the gospel.[4] Is this simply the result of diffused media that make reaching anyone with any message difficult? Or could it also be that we have neglected fundamental treasures of word, speech, and interpretation that allow us to narrate contemporary life in the light of history, tradition, and theology? As teachers and storytellers who bridge the gap between systematic theology and religious narrative, pastoral leaders must be attentive to both *what* we have to say (Scripture) and *how* we say it (interpretation). We have an opportunity to interpret the word in a way that enriches the imagination, finds universal themes in particulars, and invites the world to consider ways of living together under the gospel of the crucified and risen Christ.

What do Christians have to say to God, or to the world in the light of God? We begin with a concrete, scriptural word. Our treasure is drawn from a deep well of history, story, and chronicle. Christians engage Scripture and theology acknowledging a narrative and tradition much older and wiser than ourselves. The scriptural word offers a rich account of God and the world that both interprets contemporary life and commends a way of living.

This possibility begins with rediscovering that the word of God is not abstract and general but depicts the character of God and God's engagements with real people in real situations. Too often, Christian interpretation of the Scriptures has been communicated in ways that seem lifeless and uninspired. Our scriptural and theological treasures are not abstract but speak of the real life of persons who encounter the word of God in a particular person, the Incarnate Word.

It is hardly a coincidence that pastors and congregations who are able to speak rightly and realistically among a variety of audiences seem to have an intimate relationship with Scripture, Christian doctrine, and theological traditions. Excellent pastors understand the great figures, ideas, movements, and events of a society, but they also interpret those things alongside the common and ordinary people and places of the time. As the biblical writer told of a mighty empire by describing a group of Egyptian slaves, the pastor who is attentive to the treasures in her midst speaks of a peaceable kingdom by telling the biblical stories in the context of a faithful congregation in a local neighborhood.

4. National Clergy Survey, Pulpit & Pew Research on Pastoral Leadership, Duke Divinity School, 2001.

Similarly, the theological themes of our traditions — redemption, sin, mercy, grace — are borne on the shoulders of ordinary people and events. Clarence Jordan's "Cotton Patch" gospels and Eugene Peterson's *The Message* have offered fresh interpretations of biblical texts in this way. Poet Kathleen Norris's book *Amazing Grace: A Vocabulary of Faith* is an example of this imaginative work in a theological key. Norris blends history, theology, and story in a manner that testifies to the rich and ancient traditions that enliven our communities and point to a "word made flesh."

The difficulty of "reaching people with the gospel" may not say as much about our relationship to the world, then, as it does about our relationship to the gospel treasures. The events of September 11, 2001, brought home to many American pastors that what we have to say does not need to be clever or new. What we have to say has already been articulated in our hymns and scriptural texts. Those pastors and religious leaders who best interpreted that difficult time were men and women well acquainted with our theological traditions and biblical stories. Many of them were grounded in the daily exercise of *lectio divina,* the ancient practice of prayerful attentiveness to Scripture. In a nation struggling to comprehend what had happened, these wise pastoral leaders imaginatively offered understandable and truthful stories of hope, healing, and challenge. Their witness reminds us of the importance of reading and of encouraging engagement with these vital texts.

We have a colleague who prays each day through six psalms. Every twenty-six days, then, she begins to work her way back through the Psalms. On September 11, 2001, when asked if she had any ideas about texts that could be used in a noon prayer service, she suggested the final stanza of Psalm 44. The stanza begins, "Rouse yourself! Why do you sleep, O Lord?/Awake, do not cast us off forever!" (Ps. 44:23). It would be hard to find words more appropriate to the day, and yet we did not know to draw on them ourselves because we did not have our colleague's deep relationship with these biblical treasures.

Literature and the Arts

Christianity speaks from a tradition that is powerfully poetic. We have been shaped by verse that proclaims the word eloquently to a prosaic world. That poetry can be familiar and comforting (the Shepherd's Psalm or the angels' chorus) or subversive and scandalous (Mary's Magnificat or the Song of Songs); its verses can stir hope as well as hostility. Our sacred texts have inspired newer texts that also offer glimpses of beauty and realign our understanding of who we are and how we are to live with one another.

Poetic speech, informed and shaped by our biblical narratives, is a subversive act of profound hope. "A thing of beauty is a joy forever," as Keats said. Poetry reminds us of the Creator whose speech brought forth life. Wallace Stevens once observed, "The purpose of poetry is to contribute to man's happiness." It is hard to imagine excellent ministry that does not include a familiarity with the language, rhythm, and nuance of poetry. Certainly we have much to gain from the ancient poets, as well as contemporary poets such as Scott Cairns, Yusef Komunyakaa, Wendell Berry, Jane Kenyon, Mary Oliver, and Ruth Stone.

Denise Levertov's "The Avowal" is a beautiful and powerful reminder that the excellence to which we aspire is a gift of God's grace before it is anything else.

> As swimmers dare
> to lie face to the sky
> and water bears them,
> as hawks rest upon air
> and air sustains them,
> so would I learn to attain
> freefall, and float
> into Creator Spirit's deep embrace,
> knowing no effort earns
> that all-surrounding grace.[5]

Such poetry illumines the power of God's grace, and it calls us to discover that grace in particular patterns, rhythms, and practices of attention — to words, to our lives, to the world.

Sharing a common life schooled in our traditions is no easy task.

---

5. Denise Levertov, "The Avowal," in *The Stream and the Sapphire: Selected Poems on Religious Themes* (New York: New Directions, 1997), p. 6.

Political, cultural, and liturgical battles have increasingly fragmented the church "audience" into subcultures with few common frames of reference. The frameworks of liturgy, doctrine, and tradition that give Christian life its particular application and vigor have been disrupted. Excellence in ministry requires a recovery and renewal of those frameworks, frameworks that invite us all into Christian community, where we join the long procession that has preceded us and will follow.

Literature, drama, film, and music contribute not only to the world's conversation and culture but also to the church's. The growing interest in church-related book groups and film clubs indicates, we think, a search for meaningful narratives to share. Themes of brokenness and redemption, of death and resurrection figure in a variety of popular films and plays. As attendance at movie theaters decreases, it is interesting that church fellowship halls and sanctuaries have become places where Christians gather to explore these themes in movies like *Hotel Rwanda, In America, The Shawshank Redemption,* and even *West Side Story.* Indeed, one congregation's excellent pastor has for several years sponsored a series of five Wednesday evening discussions in February and March called "Jesus at the Oscars," in which he takes up the year's Oscar-nominated films. The gathering has steadily increased to the point where attendance now averages more than three hundred.

Similarly, book groups are a growing source of encouragement and support for Christian ministry. In contemporary texts ranging from *The Red Tent* to *Gilead, Kite Runner* to *Plainsong,* men and women of all ages are discovering a new language for interpreting and reflecting on ancient themes and traditions. Pulitzer Prize–winning novelist Oscar Hijuelos's book *Mr. Ives' Christmas* illumines in elegant prose and beautiful narration the doctrinal connections of Christmas and Easter as well as the power of ordinary Christians to embody the extraordinary grace and complexity of Christian forgiveness. Early in the story, as Edward Ives is sitting in church, the narrator observes that "Supernatural presences, invisible to the world, seemed thick in that place, as if between the image of Christ who is newly born and the image of the Christ who would die on the cross and, resurrected, return as the light of this world, there flowed a powerful, mystical energy."[6] And

6. Oscar Hijuelos, *Mr. Ives' Christmas* (New York: HarperPerennial, 1996), p. 4.

this energy, nurtured through faithful Christian practices and holy friendships, gives Ives the power and courage to forgive the young man who murdered his son. Such stories help us envision God's story in new ways, and to locate our own stories more faithfully within God's.

Just as our hymnals and Scripture remind us of the faith we sing, more contemporary singers and songwriters provide fresh glimpses into old texts. This ranges from pop and rock to classical and country and folk. For example, Carrie Newcomer's tales of "Betty's Diner" remind the listener of, and prompt the preacher to consider, the sacramental nature of common meals: *Eggs and toast like bread and wine.*[7]

While Christians often lament the biblical illiteracy of modern citizens, we should be no less concerned that our religious leaders lack rich familiarity with the diversity of wisdom, insight, and beauty nurtured through ongoing engagement with literature and the arts. This is painfully evident in leaders who speak only out of some private frame of reference, usually autobiographical — or who address only those who "speak the language" of a particular group, to the exclusion of others.

Unfortunately, many religious leaders are unfamiliar with these treasures and hence ill equipped to translate them in ways that honor the language. Poetry is the art of using words charged with their utmost meaning. Yet most pastors are encouraged neither to read poetry nor to write and speak poetically. When Wallace Stevens begins a poem by noting that "After the final no there comes a yes/And on that yes the future world depends," or when Wendell Berry closes a poignant and prophetic poem with the words "Practice resurrection," we discover far more than mere quotes for a sermon.[8] We find central conversation partners for resurrecting excellence in Christian life and leadership.

The reading and writing of poetry and prose should be integrated into the curriculum and continuing education of our seminaries and divinity schools. Funding the work of mentors who help us appreciate

7. Carrie Newcomer, "Betty's Diner," *Betty's Diner: The Best of Carrie Newcomer* (Rounder Records, 2004).

8. Wallace Stevens, "The Well Dressed Man with a Beard," in *Parts of a World* (New York: Knopf, 1942), p. 118; Wendell Berry, "Manifesto: The Mad Farmer Liberation Front," in *The Country of Marriage* (New York: Harcourt Brace Jovanovich, 1973), p. 17.

the craft and beauty of our language is as important as grants for self-renewal and reflection. Some seminaries and divinity schools already encourage the art and craft of interpretation in their curriculum; others are needed.

Our sanctuaries can become the gathering places where Christian traditions, ways of life, and forgotten customs come to life again. The architecture of our churches, the artworks, stained glass, sacred music, and texts, are signs and embodiments of the holy. We should encourage the artists among us to join their work with that of the church. There was a time when art and religion were one — think of Michelangelo's Sistine Chapel; of Milton's *Paradise Lost;* of Handel's *Messiah.* Moreover, we must encourage a theology of art, to help us deal, for example, with the (often acrimonious) aesthetic disputes over worship styles and music. It is not an either/or choice between "traditional" and "contemporary" music and worship; rather, we should be drawing from a diverse array of music and worship that honors the diversity of Christians from around the world and across the ages. The primary criterion should be what enables us to worship and praise God faithfully and beautifully.

These treasures of formation and imagination, like the treasure of holy friendships, are deeply connected and embedded in a much larger ecology. Just as artists and poets need mentors with whom to apprentice and spaces in which to learn their craft, so teachers and friends need institutions and organizations in and through which to be formed and equipped.

Institutional Treasures

Each of the authors of this book has the opportunity to begin our day with morning prayers in a chapel — one in the chapel of a divinity school, and the other in the chapel of a local congregation. We join friends, colleagues, neighbors, and strangers who come together to sing, be silent, and offer prayers of intercession. This daily ritual reminds us of the many ways we are connected to individuals and institutions who support our ministry and who seek our support. The order of prayer brings to light the abundance and variety of our shared treasures. We begin, "Together, let us pray for . . .

the people of this congregation . . .
those who suffer and those in trouble . . .
the concerns of this local community . . .
the world, its people, and its leaders . . .
the church universal — its leaders, its members, and its
    mission . . .
the communion of saints . . .

"New every morning," as one of our morning prayers begins, we discover within each category of intercessions a group that looks to us and to whom we look for encouragement, wisdom, and support. These are treasures of our ministry, including especially people who collectively create the networks and institutions that equip our ministries.

Our ministries would be less than excellent without these networks and institutions. And yet, our attention to them is often lacking. We believe it is essential that we offer both our prayer and our devotion to the healthy institutions that need to be preserved, the diminished or dispirited ones that need to be healed, the dying ones that need to be let go, and new ones waiting to be born. Before we explore these different groups, we begin with an image about institutional treasures that emerged in the strangest of places — a cattle barn.

In 1939, a Church of the Brethren relief worker named Dan West was distributing milk to hungry children during the Spanish Civil War. Distressed by the woeful inadequacy of his supply, he came to a realization: "These children don't need a cup — they need a cow." Back home in the United States, West formed Heifers for Relief with the goal of ending hunger permanently by providing families with livestock and training, sustainable means of feeding themselves.[9]

In that first effort, West shipped seventeen heifers from Pennsylvania to Puerto Rico. Families who received heifers agreed to donate the female offspring to other families, thus "passing on the gift" and gaining dignity as partners in the struggle against hunger and poverty.

Sixty years later, Heifer International is still passing on gifts,

---

9. Further information about Heifer International may be found at www .heifer.org.

working with people to determine the right kind of plants or animals for their environments, training them in the care and stewardship of those resources, and teaching them how to continue "passing on the gift" to future generations. Since the first heifers were delivered to Puerto Rico, more than 4 million families around the world have been given such gifts as a heifer, a duck, a chicken, a water buffalo, or a tree that is eventually shared with someone else. A variety of philanthropic analysts regard Heifer as one of the most influential organizations in the world.

Why do we cite an agricultural initiative when talking about the treasures of excellent ministry? We believe that Heifer embodies the activities of interpretive, visionary, and reconciling leadership we describe in Chapter 5. They have honored local tradition as a pathway to the future, taken the long view, and focused on the other's welfare rather than their own interests. They have made wise use of their authority, learned from failure, and exhibited a prophetic power that is at once judging of our failure to feed the world and gracious in offering an opportunity for reconciliation and new beginnings. They have had eyes to see and ears to hear the beauty and desire for relationship that exists among God's creation. When confronted with a global challenge, Heifer has helped create and sustain a world of smaller communities. It started with a small initiative rooted in a big idea, and now embodies a remarkable scope and ambition. We believe that our very best institutions and networks can learn from their approach.

Sustaining Institutions

Heifer's core mission to end hunger and poverty and to care for the earth has remained intact for over sixty years. Sustaining that kind of focus amid repeated and various distractions is no small feat, and one that excellent institutions can learn from. Many clergy report that the very activities that drew them to ministry are now absent from their lives. Holy friendships and excellent institutions are frequently able to rekindle and renew those crucial activities: mission, scholarship, fellowship, writing and reading, prayer and study.

The most obvious institutions that sustain pastors and congregations are colleges and universities, seminaries, and judicatories. Unfortunately, these institutions have not been exempt from the same distractions reported by clergy and congregations. Many, if not most, are burdened by shrinking membership, increased costs, and a diminished or lost sense of Christian mission and purpose. Their cultural influence has waned, and they have often found themselves competing against, rather than working alongside, one another.

And yet, these are the core institutions that provide formation, accountability, and renewal for Christian life and ministry. When colleges and universities, seminaries, and judicatories work together with congregations — for example, to support a renewed ecology of relationships for a "culture of the call" — extraordinary results begin to emerge. For too many years, Christians in the United States took for granted the ecology of institutions that nurture Christian life and help people discern their vocations for diverse lay and ordained ministries. As a result, we allowed ourselves, and our institutions, to drift away from a clear missional purpose or to settle into mediocrity.

Even so, many of the institutions that were founded and sustained by our forebears remain treasures to be sustained, renewed, and transformed — even if that involves transformations that could not have been previously anticipated. Working creatively to lead and sustain institutions is an ongoing task of Christian faithfulness, and it is particularly important in times of significant change, as we are currently experiencing. It is our responsibility and opportunity to pass them on even stronger than they are today.

In addition to these institutions, there are others that provide the kind of sustained support necessary for pastoral lives well lived: hospitals and health care institutions, clergy and family counseling centers, centers for spiritual direction, and financial planning organizations. In their own way, these institutions nurture a calling to pastoral leadership as well as sustain the personal welfare and physical wellness of religious leaders so the distractions that often derail us are minimized. Such institutions provide vital means to address concerns about clergy health — physical, emotional, and spiritual — that have significant economic and pastoral consequences for Christian ministry more generally.

Unfortunately, we have been insufficiently attentive to the kinds of support that clergy need in order to cultivate excellent physical, emotional, and spiritual health. We believe that a focus on resurrecting excellence in ministry — with attention to the significance of Christian practices that open us to the life-giving presence of God, to the nurture of holy friendships, and to a better sense of expectations of the vocation of pastoral leadership on the part of all Christians — will enhance the overall health of clergy in the United States and address some of the pathologies. But we also need to attend to sustaining those institutions and practices that support the physical wellness of pastoral leaders over time.

It is worth noting that many pastoral leaders report that they first experienced the call of God at church camp or in traveling church-music groups. Not only are these institutions critical for raising up new clergy, but they also provide a framework of support for clergy families. One pastor's child reported that the best thing about being a "PK" was that she got to see the church camp schedule before any of her peers!

Yet in a rapidly changing world, we have too often patronized or trivialized the opportunities for young people to experience the life-giving adventure of learning to feel, think, and act as faithful Christians. Newly established "youth academies" for Christian formation, many founded on seminary campuses through the support of Lilly Endowment, are providing profoundly important opportunities for young people to experience the power and excitement of Christian life. In a culture in which we too often communicate to young people that it is more challenging, and exciting, to learn how to play the piano or soccer than it is to feel, think, and act as a Christian, we need to cultivate rich ecologies for nurturing Christian faithfulness and discernment.

For example, one young woman traveled from Michigan to North Carolina for a summer youth academy at Duke Divinity School, even though her parents are not themselves practicing Christians. When she returned to her congregation, she preached a beautiful sermon about "Community and the Holy Spirit" rooted in Romans 12. After challenging the congregation to confront both personal and social challenges through a path of ongoing discernment, she observed: "If we continue down this path together, who knows where the Lord will take us? If we keep our eyes and hearts open to his Spirit, our community will continue to grow, and when we hear about communities in the Scriptures, we won't have to wonder about the extra bit of beauty, because we'll be living it."[10]

We need to pay attention to those institutions that are creatively focused on identifying, nurturing, and sustaining excellence in Christian life and ministry. Such institutions are crucial, especially at key points throughout Christian life and pastoral leadership. For example, we need to be attentive to catechesis, to forming youth and other new disciples into faithful Christians. We need to nurture young adults in the discernment of their vocations during their college years. We need to support those called to pastoral leadership during seminary and in much more extensive transitions into pastoral leadership. We then need to sustain people throughout their pastoral leadership with treasures that themselves encourage excellence. And we need to encourage renewal and transformation for those clergy who are close to being burned out in mid-vocation and find themselves "pacing toward retirement" rather than continuing to embody an ambition for the gospel.

Healing Institutions

For a variety of reasons, some institutions we once treasured have become diminished, dispirited, or broken. Some have simply outlived their purpose, others have been neglected, and a few have been abused. Sorting out why a once vibrant institution needs healing is no small effort, especially if the physician is also the patient.

There was a time in many American communities when clergy found voice and fellowship in ecumenical gatherings convened by a church federation or city-wide council of churches. As religious organizations became more diffused, the ability to gather clergy under a single umbrella for any activity became nearly impossible. Similarly, ministerial organizations that once provided encouragement and support to congregations and pastors of a particular geographical area or denominational tradition began to wane. Competing claims led clergy in a variety of directions.

Some of these ministerial organizations began to reinvent them-

10. Alexa Frye, "Community and the Holy Spirit," *Divinity* 4 (Winter 2005): 17.

selves. Clergy paid less attention to neighborhood or judicatory boundaries and more to shared interests in mission, liturgical renewal, Bible study, or preaching. Rather than holding mandatory meetings to deliver "news from headquarters," some denominations began searching for existing clergy groups and learning how to support their activities while also learning from them.

Renewing diminished or dispirited institutions requires attentiveness both to the larger culture and to potential, individual participants. A "clergy wives" group may be entirely appropriate in one location and time, but, as one of us who is married to a clergywoman once learned, neither the label nor the agenda fits in every case. Institutions that once catered to clergy and their families must now take into account two-career homes, single-parent families, aging parents, and special needs children. In the Roman Catholic tradition, some religious orders have become so small or fragmented that the notion of living "in community" seems more a recipe for loneliness than a source of sustenance. At the same time, there are places and people for whom the old models provide comfort and continuity. Deciding how much to take on and what to cast off requires agility, forgiveness, and generosity.

Hospitals and institutions of higher learning historically have provided excellent models for healing and transformation. In the early and mid-nineteenth century, America's emerging denominations started hospitals and colleges across the country. Over time, these institutions began to distance themselves from their founders. Rather than abandoning their roots, however, some of these institutions have looked for ways to incubate new relationships with their religious parents. Hospitals now work alongside neighborhood churches in creating health clinics and providing parish nurses to serve the neighborhood and congregation. Colleges that no longer provide free tuition to children of clergy families are opening their doors to collaborations for clergy sabbaticals, formation events, and mission trips.

Many of the denominational agencies that once served the publishing needs of congregations and clergy have had to renew their missions. Pastors and church members now have a variety of options for purchasing books and curriculums. Denominational loyalties no longer bind a congregation to one particular vendor. In too many cases, declining revenues and influence have led to discouragement and narrowed vision rather than creative improvisation to discover possibilities for healing and new life. Yet a new division of a publishing house, music company, or film production company can become a crucial institution for discovering new life and excitement for Christian life and ministry. Who would have thought, for example, that "Christian rock" and gospel musicians such as Amy Grant would discover such large audiences, or that Mel Gibson's *The Passion of the Christ* would generate blockbuster revenues? Christians may have differing opinions about the cultural and theological merits of these phenomena, but it is clear that they represent a bold new way of envisioning Christian media.

Typically, those organizations that are finding renewed life have transcended established bureaucracies and even judicatory boundaries. They have availed themselves of modern technologies while holding on to established purpose and vision. Like the villager that "passes on the gift," these organizations are finding ways to return a portion of their revenues to support further the significance of Christian purpose and mission.

Letting Go and Raising Up

The most difficult decisions are those that require a letting go of once-vibrant programs or institutions that must now be pruned or weeded to make way for a new thing. Certain degree programs within colleges, universities, and seminaries are no longer flourishing. Clergy who once pursued a Doctor of Ministry not so much for the title but for the opportunity to learn and study with peers are finding new institutions that provide such learning with less expense. Local congregations whose purpose and mission within an evolving neighborhood have become irrelevant have closed so that new ones with fresh vision might arise in their place. Similar challenges face some colleges, church camps, and other religious institutions. On a larger cultural scale, we can think of how in the United States orphanages have given way to "children's homes" as family patterns and judgments about how best to care for needy children have changed.

Whether we are sustaining excellent institutions, healing broken ones, or raising up new ones where others have died, several questions seem worth considering. First, are these institutions rooted in a shared and expressed need of clergy, congregations, and the broader ecology of Christians? Excellent pastors frequently arise from vibrant, excellent congregations. Institutions that intend to support one must be attentive to both. The cultures in which clergy serve reflect and shape shared expressions of ministry.

Second, who are the collaborating partners? Heifer International claims that they "can't imagine working without our partners," which seems like pretty sound advice to us. Just as good physical, mental, and spiritual health are related, there are crucial connections among networks and agencies that support and equip congregations and clergy.

Third, is this institution duplicating an already existing organization, and if so, why? Several years ago one of us worked with a local congregation eager to provide a children's daycare center for parishioners and neighbors. Several months of work had been put into the effort when participants called a halt to the project because of low registration. The congregation thought it had carefully studied its environment but later learned that there were multiple childcare centers in the neighborhood and increasingly fewer children. What they also learned was that there was an unmet need for adult daycare, which they then went on to meet. Sustaining old institutions and creating new ones requires an honest assessment of the needs of the clergy, congregations, and communities being served, of whether there is room for collaboration, and of whether partnerships would benefit everyone involved.

Fourth, one of the critical questions facing any institution is how dependent that organization is willing to be on short-term, limited funding. Just as funders must struggle with which strategies and activities merit continuation, funded institutions must struggle with long-term sustainability. Ken Carder, director of Lilly Endowment's Sustaining Pastoral Excellence program, urges funded institutions to avoid preoccupation with presumptions of scarcity as articulated in the question, "How can we get the money to survive?" Instead, he urges them to explore the signs of God's abundant, empowering grace already at work in their programs. Carder urges these institutions who are promoting a culture of pastoral excellence to sustain their momentum by looking to "imagination rooted in God's abundance, stories of changed lives and communities, and cooperative connections and partnerships."[11]

Finally, institutions supportive of excellence must articulate and strive for an eschatological vision, a sense that our lives and ministries, and thus also our institutions, are moving toward the fullness of God's kingdom. Heifer International envisions "communities living together in peace and equitably sharing the resources of a healthy planet." Resurrecting excellence requires a vision that sees beyond immediate budget or institutional necessities to the time when "God shall wipe away all tears . . . , and there shall be no more death" (Rev. 21:4 KJV). How do our supporting institutions give clergy, their families, their congregations, and the surrounding communities a glimpse of such a peaceable kingdom?

Perhaps the only grace greater than receiving a gift is being able to pass a gift along to others. Institutions are treasures that can be multiplied and sustained over time; they can be developed with a sense of ambitious scale and scope that can benefit God's people in beautiful, powerful, life-giving ways. But they require our faithful attention and care. And — always viewed from the perspective of such attention and care, and in the light of God's transforming abundance — they require money.

Economic Treasures

Pastor Carole Brown is serving her second church since graduating from her denomination's flagship seminary nearly ten years ago. The last four years as a solo pastor in this county-seat community have been extremely satisfying. The church membership has grown modestly, several new mission projects have been initiated in the last year, and even Carole's family life has improved, since her husband now has only a ten-mile commute to work rather than the hour-long drive he endured in her last congregation. Carole enjoys the weekly rhythms of preaching, education, and pastoral care.

11. Kenneth L. Carder, "Life after the Lilly Grants? Sustaining Momentum for Pastoral Excellence," Sustaining Pastoral Excellence Web site, http://www.divinity.duke.edu/programs/spe/articles/200507/carder.html.

Carole was an associate pastor in her previous church and would have been happy to remain on the staff of a larger congregation, but the cost of keeping two full-time associate pastors was increasingly a struggle for the church. Carole's supervising pastor told her nearly a year in advance that if giving didn't improve, the church would probably eliminate her position. No one was happy about the prospect of losing her, but pension and insurance costs simply outpaced congregational giving. The year before Carole left, personnel costs accounted for nearly two-thirds of the church's operating budget.

As she prepares for her fifth year in this setting, Carole intends to ask for either a summer sabbatical or a modest pay raise. She doesn't feel that she can ask for both. The church has been very supportive in providing a discount for her daughter to attend the church's preschool. The congregation also is replete with gardeners, doting grandmothers, and retired men in search of a church- or home-repair project. Carole feels well loved and appreciated. She also knows that her pay is as much as, or more than, that of many of the people in her congregation, and certainly more than those in the larger community. Compared with many other pastors she knows, Carole is very satisfied in her work, and she would like to remain in this congregation for several more years.

Carole's satisfaction is important to her husband, Richard — but he also reminds her that she is the same age and has as much formal education as the two attorneys on her personnel committee, who bring home salaries at least four times as large as hers. Without Richard's salary, they would not have paid off their student loans as quickly, nor would they have been able to help Carole's family with additional expenses incurred after her father's stroke. The denomination of which Carole is a member paid for over half of her seminary expenses in exchange for her promise that she would serve in this particular area for at least five years. After graduating from college with nearly $20,000 in loans, she was happy to make that promise, although she and Richard had a long discussion about whether they wanted to be tied to a particular area, since Richard's opportunities for career advancement depended somewhat on his being geographically flexible.

As Richard and Carole think about their future, they question whether they will remain at this church as long as Carole now hopes.

They are already saving for their daughter's college expenses, and they have agreed that they would not be able to count on the "preacher's kid" discount that many colleges used to offer. Carole loves her ministry, and the congregation loves her. She is a strong leader in her local community and in her denomination. Carole is a happy pastor. The congregation hopes she will remain. But they both know that the day is coming when they will have to make some hard choices.

Defining "Necessities"

As you might guess, Carole Brown is a composite character. We invented her identity, but we have met many pastors, congregations, and judicatories who share her story. Good and faithful pastors who are essentially satisfied with their work but who struggle with how to provide for their families. Gracious and giving congregations who desire wise pastoral leadership but whose shrinking membership and old buildings oblige them to make choices about things like roof replacement and insurance costs. Judicatory leaders who lie awake at night and wonder if they are about to face the perfect storm: shrinking membership, aging buildings, unhealthy but long-living clergy.

In all fairness, we should not overlook the fact that clergy compensation has been a topic of discussion since the first pastors and the first congregations settled in the new world. According to historian James Hudnut-Beumler, pastors have long complained about being underpaid, and laity similarly have grumbled about the poor quality of pastoral leadership.[12] How we address these perennial concerns is a matter of caution. It would be too easy — but also not too far off target — to suggest that there may be an inherent tension between the economics of ministry and the theology of ministry.

The Pulpit & Pew 2001 National Clergy Survey offers some important initial insights. First, while it is true that most clergy are generally satisfied in their ministry, those who report low levels of satisfaction, and particularly those who have considered leaving the ministry, frequently cite inadequate salary and benefits as a determining fac-

---

12. See James Hudnut-Beumler, *God's Gold: American Protestants, Their Churches and Their Money* (Chapel Hill: University of North Carolina Press, forthcoming).

tor.[13] The study further reports that a Protestant pastor's reluctance to talk about salary is often matched by a spouse's lack of reluctance to express concern. Many of these spouses also work outside the home, sometimes just to help make ends meet, and always contributing to the family income, raising questions about whether or not a pastor is free to accept a new appointment or call because of the spouse's vocation and income.

Since most Protestant clergy secure loans to pay for their undergraduate and/or seminary education (or, in the case of second-career clergy, cash in on retirement plans to do so), the burden of debt weighs on pastors from the time they arrive at their first parish. Anxieties about those debts continue as clergy families consider how to provide a college education for their children and retirement savings for themselves. Compounding the concern is a reluctance on the part of most clergy to discuss salary issues with a personnel or supervisory group.

Congregations and judicatories also are stretched financially. The financial and material disparity between smaller and larger churches is significant. While most American Christians attend medium to large churches, the majority of congregations are small: more than half of the congregations in the country have fewer than 75 members. Those smaller congregations that once employed a seminary graduate are now struggling to pay their heating bill, let alone the pension and insurance costs of a seminary graduate. Judicatories, in turn, are questioning whether they have an oversupply of theologically trained clergy, an undersupply of personnel who can affordably staff these smaller congregations, or too many congregations that are no longer viable.

Any response to this emerging crisis — and an increasing number of clergy, congregations, and judicatories seem to believe that a perfect storm is developing — must take into account the current realities of a culture shaped by free-market economic assumptions and establish a clear theological framework for moving ahead. One without the other is sure to intensify the peril.

---

13. For a thorough examination of the data on clergy salaries and compensation, see the Pulpit & Pew 2001 National Clergy Survey, as reported and interpreted in Jackson Carroll, *God's Potters: Pastoral Leadership and the Shaping of Congregations* (Grand Rapids: Eerdmans, 2006).

The market economy inhabited by American Christians is no longer only a system for the exchange of goods and services. It has become a solution to basic human problems and a source of penultimate (and sometimes ultimate) meaning and fulfillment.[14] While some may desire a different economic system, we proceed with the assumption that for now we must navigate the turbulent capitalist waters rather than fashion a whole new sea. One of the current realities is that a free market system will shape the choices that pastors, congregations, and judicatories make. If congregations can no longer afford full-time, ordained clergy, they will look to other means to meet their needs. Already, many congregations are replacing ordained staff members with part-time and full-time lay leadership who are trained either within the congregation or in alternative educational and formational programs.

We also must acknowledge that the American economy has, over time, increasingly shaped a population that believes "more is better."[15] Wealth and poverty are relative terms, based on a comparison with others. A pastor who believes she is "just making it" may be regarded by another, lesser-paid pastor as living with considerable means. Satisfaction in our economy is likely always to be countercultural. What is "enough" will often be perceived only in comparative terms.[16]

We are not suggesting that Christian communities simply capitulate to the market economy. There are congregations and pastors who have cultivated alternative economies within the larger market, and we should be learning from them. For instance, we have heard reports of clergy who pool their salaries and distribute the income as members have need. These strategies take into account the size of a family,

14. We are grateful to Bishop Kenneth L. Carder for his perspective on the role of the American economic market in pastoral compensation. For a more complete analysis, see Carder, "Ministry as Commodity," in Becky R. McMillan and Matthew J. Price, *How Much Should We Pay the Pastor? A Fresh Look at Clergy Salaries*, Pulpit & Pew Research Reports (Winter 2003), pp. 24-25.

15. For a more complete description of this "culture of desire," see Robert Wuthnow's *Poor Richard's Principle* (Princeton, N.J.: Princeton University Press, 1996) and economist Robert Frank's *Luxury Fever* (Princeton, N.J.: Princeton University Press, 1999).

16. Thanks to Chris Coble for helping us more closely examine these economic assumptions.

the stage and transition of children or aging parents, and the intangible economic support that may be available in one location but not another. We should learn from these and other communities by asking what they have learned, what challenges they have faced, and how they sustain their efforts.

As we confront the larger economy in which most of us operate, we believe an important first step is to construct a clear theological framework for thinking about economics and Christian life generally. An excellent starting point for thinking about Christian life would be Proverbs 30:7-9:

> Two things I ask of you;
>   do not deny them to me before I die:
> Remove far from me falsehood and lying;
>   give me neither poverty nor riches;
>   feed me with the food that I need,
> or I shall be full, and deny you,
>   and say, "Who is the LORD?"
> or I shall be poor, and steal,
>   and profane the name of my God.

Both too much and too little wealth is tempting. Too much wealth, and we come to believe in the myth of self-sufficiency. Too little, and we are tempted to steal to satisfy our basic needs. The challenge is to find some consensus on what constitutes the necessities of life. Ken Carder reminds us that in the early Methodist movement, John Wesley "expected the preachers to be financially supported so as to provide necessities of life for their families. Wesley defined 'necessities' as *sufficient* food, *decent* clothing, and *proper* housing. Although *sufficient, decent,* and *proper* are relative criteria, the emphasis was on adequacy of provision and not on status or competition or reward."[17]

While some judicatories already provide "minimum" standards for salary and housing, we wonder if these standards are based entirely on the local economic market (such as regional cost of living indices) or whether they take into account the local theological measures of sufficient, decent, and proper. Congregations and local

17. Carder, "Ministry as Commodity," p. 24.

judicatories may well want to examine the operating budget of the church as well as discuss the family budgets and personal accounts of constituents in order to better articulate sufficiency. Pastoral salaries dramatically above or significantly below the means of the gathered community raise important questions about life together.

The burden of defining "necessities" does not rest, of course, entirely upon the congregation or judicatory. We know very little about the economic assumptions clergy bring to their ministries. Are there significant differences in a theology of personal and vocational economics between younger, recently graduated seminarians and older, second-career pastors? What roles do class, race, geography, and ecclesiology play in shaping assumptions about pastoral salaries and household economics? Pastors and congregations may be able to shape larger denominational policies as they more intentionally and fully address the issues of their local economies.

Beyond the cash salary that clergy need to survive or even thrive, we should address more broadly the material realities and treasures that are important to pastoral lives well lived. This includes provision for access to the treasures described above, opportunities for travel and other cultural enrichment, and provision for children's education and for retirement. We need to provide appropriate "micro-economies" that will sustain excellent ministry and pastoral leadership in diverse and particular contexts in relation to well-articulated theological convictions, broader cultural expectations, and economic realities. This has implications for congregations and pastors themselves, for judicatories, for colleges and seminaries and other institutions of the church that nurture pastoral leaders, and for related institutions that play a significant role in either enhancing or diminishing the economics of ministry and pastoral leadership.

Addressing Economic Challenges

As we seek to better understand and develop the kinds of economic treasures that are necessary for Christian pastoral ministry well lived, several strategies present themselves for consideration. First, it is important to be able to articulate in powerful and persuasive ways why formal theological education for pastoral ministry is crucial, and why it is so expensive. Both pastors and congregational members are heard to ask, "Is a theological degree necessary in order to pastor a church?" We hope that by now readers will sense and understand our profound commitment to theological education. But we also recognize that "learning ministry" takes many forms and continually needs to be re-formed and reimagined in order to meet the needs of particular traditions and locations as well as economies.

For instance, a variety of Protestant and Roman Catholic traditions have historically emphasized the role of well-trained laity who are provided with support and oversight by an ordained pastor with sacramental presence. The pastor of a larger congregation might oversee a cluster of smaller congregations, whose day-to-day ministry is carried out by the laity. Theological education for these lay ministers is currently extended from the ordained pastor's own formation and education and further complemented by judicatory-related staff or pastors who share the teaching role. But there might be other ways to enhance the formative education of lay pastors and, in the Roman Catholic tradition, lay ecclesial ministers.

Considerable discussion and work also needs to take place around the question of who is responsible for the financial support of ministerial candidates. Congregational support of denominational seminaries is declining as local churches make choices between paying the light bill and paying denominational dues. As congregations continue to move from hiring ordained staff to non-ordained, the perceived obligation and relationship to seminaries and divinity schools is weakened. The immediate "benefit" to the local congregation becomes less obvious. As we have already said, there is a growing need for congregations, seminaries, and judicatories to make connections that strengthen their collective and individual missions. It is unfair to ministerial candidates, and to the churches to which they will be appointed, to saddle them with educational debt on the front end of ministry, offer them low salaries as they practice ministry, and (in the case of Protestants) provide fewer options for supporting a family, educating children, and planning for retirement as they move toward older adulthood.

We believe that becoming far more articulate about the dynamics of institutions — creating and sustaining, healing and renovating, letting go and raising up — will enable American Christians to use our economic resources more wisely. In too many cases, people have been unwilling either to make difficult decisions about when an institution needs to die or be transformed, or to explore creative possibilities for long-term sustenance and renewal. Too often a short-term focus has minimized current costs only to defer the problems to a later time. Learning to value institutions and to attend to them in all of their complexity is crucial to addressing the economic challenges of Christian ministry in the United States.

Further, if the costs associated with aging buildings, health insurance, and pension plans continue to dominate the decisions about how our money is spent, we must find new and creative ways to control them. Many congregations have begun to share their building space, and its expenses, with other organizations in ways that enhance the missions of both. One of us lives a few blocks from a large, older congregation that has restored its building and renewed its ministry by transforming part of the building into art studios and a gallery that serves members and neighbors. The members have drawn on their tradition's long engagement with the arts as the foundation and substance for their outreach. Contributions for renovation and renewal have allowed the church to increase the number of staff as well as their ministry programs while distributing the costs of maintenance and renovation among a variety of constituents.

Similarly, the aging and wellness of our clergy cannot be ignored. We will always need a mix of older and younger clergy, but the growing costs of an aging clergy population cannot be supported financially by the small number of younger clergy entering vocational ministry. Clergy, congregations, and judicatories share insurance and pension costs. We need new ways to reduce these costs by offering larger numbers of participants. In local economies, this may mean insurance plans that cross denominational boundaries.

American Christians are increasingly aware that "clergy health" is a serious issue that needs to be addressed. But we are convinced that it is a mistake to see the costs of health insurance as only a narrowly defined economic problem. Loneliness among clergy has contributed to a high dependence on prescription drugs, especially antidepressants. The stresses of conflicting expectations among congregations, pastors, and judicatories often lead to unhealthy patterns of behavior. By contrast, the discovery of vital friendships, a sense of fulfilling vocation,

and rich Christian practices (including Sabbath-keeping) often are cor-
related with pastors attending to their health and receiving encouragement to do so. We are convinced that resurrecting excellence in pastoral leadership is a crucial dimension of improving the health of clergy
in the United States. But so also is careful attentiveness to the challenges of health insurance that are shared among diverse vocations
and, indeed, the entire United States.

The Carole Browns of our communities provide faithful, wise pastoral leadership. Supporting these pastors and congregations requires
us to face a variety of important questions: What are the financial and
material treasures necessary to equip pastors, as well as their families,
for excellent ministry? How can local congregations working collectively and individually provide those resources in ways that are appropriate to the local economy? What will be the role of denominational
and other institutions in supporting the conception, development,
and implementation of these strategies? How can we draw on the
abundance of financial wealth among Christians in the United States
to support and sustain excellence in ministry, the networks of institutions that enable excellent ministry to be formed, nurtured, and to
flourish over time, and the arts that stir our imaginations and enable
us to behold the beauty that connects us in fresh ways to God?

Enhancing Economic Treasures

We suspect that a lack of imagination about the economics of congregations and pastoral ministry has been confused with a lack of financial
resources. The level of financial support necessary to equip excellent
pastoral ministry is already available in many of our congregations, and
if we look creatively at the potential for wealthier congregations to
partner with poorer ones, there is significant wealth among American
Christians that has barely been tapped. There is also more than enough
wealth to create, renovate, sustain, and extend the ecologies and networks of institutions that can enable excellent ministries and pastors
to flourish. Not only do we have an opportunity to ask for support; we
have an obligation to engage the narratives and dreams of others who
are capable of sustaining Christian excellence. In her poem *Aurora
Leigh,* Elizabeth Barrett Browning writes:

God answers sharp and sudden on some prayers,
And thrusts the thing we have prayed for in our face,
A gauntlet with a gift in't.[18]

Sometimes the challenges we face are the gifts yet to be recognized.

There are people of wealth in many of our congregations and judicatories whose lives have been transformed by excellent clergy and congregations but who have never been asked to "pass on the gift" through their own ideas and resources. Further, there are significant resources in philanthropic institutions — large foundations, smaller family foundations, as well as newer foundations that have been formed from the assets of institutions that no longer exist, such as hospitals and colleges — that need to be invited and challenged to become more strategic and creative in addressing the ecology of pastoral leadership in its complexity and significance. As we write this book, people throughout the United States are describing the tremendous transfer of wealth that is anticipated to occur over the next two decades. The numbers are staggering.

We have referred in earlier chapters to the passage in 1 Timothy 6:19 that invites Christians to "take hold of the life that really is life." It is important to note that this passage concludes a section challenging those who place their confidence in riches rather than God. The full passage of 1 Timothy 6:17-19 reads as follows: "As for those who in the present age are rich, command them not to be haughty, or to set their hopes on the uncertainty of riches, but rather on God who richly provides us with everything for our enjoyment. They are to do good, to be rich in good works, generous, and ready to share, thus storing up for themselves the treasure of a good foundation for the future, so that they may take hold of the life that really is life." Too often, the problem is not so much a shortage of economic resources as it is a lack of faithful interpretation, of vision and ambition for the gospel, and of willingness to engage in the accountability and support that mark ministries of reconciliation. In such contexts, and especially as we anticipate such a dramatic transfer of wealth in the United States, the challenge is to cultivate pastoral leaders who are gifted interpreters,

---

18. Elizabeth Barrett Browning, *Aurora Leigh*, book 2 (New York: C. S. Francis, 1860), p. 70.

visionaries, and reconcilers, people with an ambition for the gospel who also are gifted at crafting imaginative strategies that make a transformative difference.

We believe that there are institutions and institutional leaders who can further cultivate the ecology of a well-lived pastoral life who have not yet been invited to share their work and ideas. And, we would emphasize, these include institutions, leaders, and others who may seem to possess little wealth or substance. While called to be generous with those who have needs, we are also called to be attentive to those who have gifts we have not yet discovered.

"For where your treasure is, there your heart will be also" (Matthew 6:21). There are profound treasures available, and necessary, to support and sustain excellent ministry. We need to be attentive to those treasures, caring for them and seeking to deepen and extend them. If we — laity and clergy alike — cultivate an ambition for the gospel shaped by a commitment to resurrecting excellence, we will develop eyes to see and ears to hear the God who, working within us, is able to accomplish abundantly far more than all we can ask or imagine.

Coda

After a very long day of what felt like feeble efforts at living a life "worthy of the gospel," a song on the radio suddenly sounded like a prayer:

> I laid in bed that night and thought about the day
> And how my life is like a roller coaster ride
> The ups and downs and crazy turns along the way
> It'll throw you off if you don't hold on tight
> You can't really smile until you've shed some tears
> I could die today or I might live on for years
>
> I love this crazy, tragic,
> Sometimes almost magic,
> Awful, beautiful life.[1]

At the beginning and end of every day, we offer our ministries and ourselves to God. Sometimes those offerings seem inconsequential, certainly less than excellent: long meetings, lingering disagreements, unhappy interruptions. But they also hold glimpses of beauty and vitality: a circle of friends singing for those silenced by grief, a subtle but extravagant gesture that invites reconciliation, an intrusion of grace that rekindles hope, the discovery of a new friend in Christ. We

---

1. Darryl Worley, "Awful, Beautiful Life," *Darryl Worley* (Dreamworks Nashville, 2004).

are accountable for our offerings, but it is God's resurrecting excellence that accounts for the promise that our "ups and downs and crazy turns along the way" are part of an all-encompassing beauty and vitality that is not yet fully revealed. Our uncertain offerings and God's extravagant faithfulness blend into a vocation that can be described as an "awful, beautiful life."

We have tried to be candid about the murmurings, failings, and heartbreak that occur within Christian communities and the pastoral life. We know all too well the stories of individuals and communities who have been wounded or marginalized by the mediocrity, malice, or misconduct of Christian laity and clergy. Excellence is threatened by inattentiveness to these tragedies and unwillingness to deal squarely with the consequences of such attitudes and behaviors. But we also believe that all around us are glimpses of the "everlasting holy places." The stories and testimonies of our friends who helped shape this book demonstrate our conviction. We hope that our readers' ambition for the gospel is renewed as they gain new eyes for seeing how the life, death, and resurrection of Jesus are both the basis and the goal of our shared summons to excellence.

There is a paradox to the excellence we commend, a both/and rather than an either/or. We affirm that the Christian life can be both awful and beautiful, both tragic and hopeful, both joined with the saints and engaged with the world. Resurrecting excellence is cultivated by Christians and their communities who determinedly live at these intersections and are willing to be interrupted by the people, sacraments, and Christian practices that remind us of the "breadth and length and height and depth" of Christ's love for the world.

Sustaining this excellence requires the capacity for measuring life by the complexities of judgment and grace. Such discernment begins with a clarity of vocation and a willingness to wrestle with the distortions that can emerge when a lifelong commitment to faith is clouded by urgent, but not necessarily important, distractions. Ultimately, this "awful, beautiful life" is manifest wherever the borders between heaven and earth fade and the vocation of a particular people in a particular time and place shines forth with the reflected light of Christ. We hope to have encouraged vital Christian discipleship among faithful communities, as well as gifted pastoral leadership that inspires, nurtures, and challenges those communities and indeed all of us who care about the beauty and excellence of God.

The Capacity to See and Hear God's Resurrecting Excellence

We want to conclude with one last vignette from the journal of John Ames, pastor of a Congregational church in Marilynne Robinson's fictional town of Gilead. Ames reflects on an encounter with a young couple strolling down the street:

> The sun had come up brilliantly after a heavy rain, and the trees were glistening and very wet. On some impulse, plain exuberance, I suppose, the fellow jumped up and caught hold of a branch, and a storm of luminous water came pouring down on the two of them, and they laughed and took off running, the girl sweeping water off her hair and her dress as if she were a little bit disgusted, but she wasn't. It was a beautiful thing to see, like something from a myth. I don't know why I thought of that now, except perhaps because it is easy to believe in such moments that water was made primarily for blessing, and only secondarily for growing vegetables or doing the wash. I wish I had paid more attention to it. My list of regrets may seem unusual, but who can know that they are, really. This is an interesting planet. It deserves all the attention you can give it.[2]

Attention to God's presence in the world, a gift for seeing water as blessing before it is used for anything else — Ames sees the grace of God in the ordinary beauty of daily life.

Ames believes in extravagant beauty. It is the beauty of God, of God's grace, of God's presence in the world, of God's healing and redeeming love. That belief leads John Ames to see beauty in the ordinary blessings of life, and it leads him to take the risk of blessing a prodigal whom he struggles to love. At the very end of the novel, and at the conclusion of John Ames's ministry, he notes: "Theologians talk

2. Marilynne Robinson, *Gilead* (New York: Farrar, Straus & Giroux, 2004), pp. 27-28.

about a prevenient grace that precedes grace itself and allows us to accept it. I think there must also be a prevenient courage that allows us to be brave — that is, to acknowledge that there is more beauty than our eyes can bear, that precious things have been put into our hands and to do nothing to honor them is to do great harm. And therefore, this courage allows us, as the old men said, to make ourselves useful. It allows us to be generous, which is another way of saying exactly the same thing."[3]

There is so much more to the Christian life than we ever take the time to see, or that is ever fully revealed to us. But we are heirs of One who "pioneers and perfects" our ability to see and hear differently (see Heb. 12:2). That legacy and the attending treasures are often discovered at the intersections that reflect not only the shape of the cross but the life of the one who died on it and lives again. Our faithfulness is a call to see deeply.

William Stafford's poem "Ask Me" is a reminder of how the hidden currents of God's grace reside at nearly every "crazy turn" of our life:

> Some time when the river is ice ask me
> mistakes I have made. Ask me whether
> what I have done is my life. Others
> have come in their slow way into
> my thought, and some have tried to help
> or to hurt: ask me what difference
> their strongest love or hate has made.
>
> I will listen to what you say.
> You and I can turn and look
> at the silent river and wait. We know
> the current is there, hidden; and there
> are comings and goings from miles away
> that hold the stillness exactly before us.
> What the river says, that is what I say.[4]

3. Robinson, *Gilead*, p. 246.

4. William Stafford, "Ask Me," in *Stories That Could Be True: New and Collected Poems* (New York: Harper & Row, 1977), p. 19.

A Heart for Resurrecting Excellence

In 1986, the United Methodist Council of Bishops sent American Bishop David Lawson to Liberia at the height of the Liberian civil war. Bishop Lawson's job was to help keep his Liberian colleague, Bishop Arthur Kulah, out of jail. Lawson also was asked to visit other Liberian pastors who had been incarcerated and to seek their freedom. "That's all that was asked of me," Bishop Lawson remarks with a wry smile.

The second day he was there, Bishop Kulah's assistant invited Lawson on a three-and-a-half-hour drive outside the city. When they arrived, Bishop Lawson followed his guide up a hill to a patch of ground where a square plot was formed by evergreens. In the middle of the plot was a small, square, concrete box. There was nothing ornate about the unmarked box. No inscriptions, nothing to indicate what it was.

The bishop stood silently beside his host, who quietly wept while looking at the box. Finally Bishop Lawson broke the silence and gently asked what they were looking at.

"You don't know the story?" his host asked. "This is a story of the Fadleys, a young couple who were American seminary graduates and missionaries to Liberia. He was an agriculturalist, sent to teach Liberians how to grow crops from this arid land. She was a teacher who started schools in many of the surrounding territories. The people here fell in love with the Fadleys, and they fell in love with the Liberians."

Eventually, the wife began to fall weak. The doctors couldn't find what was wrong with her and suggested that they return to the States for a better examination. But the Fadleys lingered. There were crops to plant, schools to start, congregations that were arising from their work. This was home.

Mrs. Fadley eventually became so weak that she couldn't travel even if she wanted to. At the end of her life, she asked her husband for one last favor. "We've loved these people," she said. "What we've been doing is beautiful and important. Our hearts belong here. When I die you can ship my body home. My parents would want that. But first I want you to ask the surgeons to remove my heart. I want my heart here."

At that moment, Bishop Lawson knew what was in the box. "I knew I was on holy ground. I stood there silently beside this weeping assistant, and all I could think about was whether there was any group, any place, any people in this world that I should regard as so important and beautiful that I would want to bury my heart in that place, among those people."[5]

We are not suggesting that an excellence shaped by the life, death, and resurrection of Jesus Christ requires faithful Christians and pastors to nail themselves to the cross. We do believe that resurrecting excellence is fundamentally shaped by a lifelong attentiveness and obedience to the life, death, and resurrection of Jesus Christ.

A single-hearted, single-minded ambition for the gospel will eventually ask one fundamental question of us all: Is there any group, any place, any people that you see as so important and beautiful in the economy of God that you are willing to bury your heart in that place, among those people, as together you pursue the beauty and excellence of God?

Looking Back . . . and Ahead

The final stages of writing this book coincidentally — or perhaps, not — converge with its authors' twentieth anniversary as seminary graduates. Our friendship was cultivated in that place, and our vocation was awakened by, and nourished in, a community shaped by distinct practices of prayer, worship, and study. There we were introduced to the beauty and vitality of the Christian life as well as the murmurings, failings, and heartbreak that can also mark the gathered company of the faithful. Along the way, we have been nurtured and held accountable by the "cloud of witnesses" and holy friends who share the hope of this "crazy, tragic, . . . awful, beautiful life." When we have been willing to watch and listen, we have been strengthened by their wisdom and inspired to respond with our own faithful witness to the resurrecting excellence of God. In short, if we had it to do all over again . . . we would.

5. Thanks to United Methodist Bishop David Lawson for sharing this story with us.

Index

accountability, 61, 64-65, 74, 76, 98, 101, 169
administration, gift of, 107-8, 118
alongside, ministry as, 60, 69, 77
Amazing Grace: A Vocabulary of Faith (Norris), 146
Ambrose, 116-17
Ames, John, 8-9, 173
Antioch Christian Church (southern Indiana), 15-16
Apostles' Creed, 13-15
apprenticeship in pastoral training, 106, 116, 124-26
art: pastoral ministry as, 30, 117; and religion, 150
"Ask Me" (Stafford), 174
athletics imagery, 52-53, 57
Augustine, 51, 106, 144
Aurora Leigh (Browning), 168
authoritarian leadership, 91, 98
authority, use of, 26, 97, 107, 134-36, 152
"Avowal, The" (Levertov), 147

Balaam's donkey, 135
baptism, 10-11, 30-31, 48, 50, 63-64, 68, 72, 105, 114, 138
Baptism, Eucharist, and Ministry, 79n.1
Bartlett, David, 81n.4

Bass, Dorothy, 58
beauty: of God, 8, 13, 15, 17, 21-22, 50, 173; in literature, 147, 149; in ministry, 7-9, 12, 15, 19-21, 61, 96, 98, 125
Beazley, Hamilton, 108n.34
Bernard of Clairvaux, 20n.22
Berry, Wendell, 54, 149
Bonhoeffer, Dietrich, 44, 99-100
book groups, 148
Breathing Space (Neumark), 9
Broadway Christian Parish (South Bend, Ind.), 69-70
brokenness, 22-23, 38, 40, 42, 63, 71-72, 128, 136
Brown, Michael, 55
Browning, Elizabeth Barrett, 168
Byrne, Jane, 46

Cabrini-Green housing project, 46-47
Caleb, 132
calling, 101-2, 109, 153-54; and the gift of attentiveness, 103-4; understanding of ordained ministry as, 80, 82-84, 88-93
Calvin, John, 8
Carder, Ken, 36-37, 43, 49, 57n.10, 131, 158, 163n.14, 164

gifts, spiritual, 6-7, 16, 41, 47, 65, 98-103; for pastoral leadership, 81, 84, 98, 102
Gilead (Robinson), 8
God: beauty of, 8, 13, 15, 17, 21-22, 50, 173; and gift of friendship, 63-65, 69, 71; love of, 1, 15, 38-39, 62, 113; and Scripture, 144-45
God Struck Me Dead (Johnson), 40
God Without Being (Marion), 106
golden calf, 135
Goodman, Andrew, 36
Good to Great (Collins), 2
Graham, Billy, 54
Grant, Amy, 157
Great Commandment, 51, 52n.4
Great Commission, 105-6
Gregory of Nazianzus, 117
Gregory of Nyssa, 51
Gregory the Great, 23, 30, 42-43, 53, 80, 86, 108, 117, 121
Gutiérrez, Gustavo, 54

Harvard College, 85, 111
Hauerwas, Stanley, 26
health insurance, 161-62, 167-68
Heaney, Seamus, 136
Heifer International, 151-52, 158-59
high church, 80-81, 88
Hijuelos, Oscar, 148
Hildegard of Bingen, 40
holiness, 4, 42, 53; as expected of clergy, 23, 80, 86-87, 92, 96-97, 98n.26, 107, 109, 127
Holy Family Lutheran Church (Chicago), 46-48
Holy Spirit, 20-23, 40, 42, 49-50, 53, 56, 63-64, 83, 96, 103, 113, 131-32
Hopkins, Gerard Manley, 7
hospitality, 54-56, 61, 68-70, 101, 130, 143
hospitals, 156, 169
Hudnut-Beumler, James, 161
humility, 3, 17, 92, 97

Hunter, Leslie, 46

Idea of a University, The (Newman), 112
illness, terminal, 14-15
imagination, pastoral, 122-25
immigrants, 11-12
improvisational theater, terms from, 126, 137-39
individualism, 60, 62-63, 93
Infelt, Charles, 46-47
institutional treasures of ministry, 143-44, 150-59
institutions, 127-28, 166-68; governance of, by interpreters, 128-32; governance of, by reconcilers, 128-29, 136-39; governance of, by visionaries, 128-29, 132-36; healing and renewing, 155-57; raising up, 157-59; sustaining, 152-55
interpreters, pastors as, 128, 130-32
intersections, 28-31, 48; of church and world, 46-47; of community and solitude, 43-45; of strength and weakness, 39-43; of tragedy and hope, 35-39, 43; of young and old, 31-35

Jennings, Willie James, 115
Jerome, 50
Jesus Christ: death and resurrection of, 12-13, 39, 90-93, 101; as example to follow, 3, 17-21, 29, 86, 97-98, 116, 140; friendships of, 75, 78; hospitality of, 68, 143; solitude sought by, 43-45; teachings of, 7, 71, 90, 97, 138
John Paul II, 54
Johnson, Barry, 137n.27
Johnson, James Weldon, 105
Jones, L. Gregory, 114n.4, 119n.11
Jordan, Clarence, 146
Joshua, 132